Not known, because not looked for
But heard, half heard, in the stillness
Between two waves of the sea.
Quick now,
Here, now
Always –
A condition of complete simplicity
(costing not less than everything)

FOUR QUARTETS, THOMAS STEARNS ELIOT

FOR DISCUSSION CONSIDER THIS

NO OTHER WAY NOW

Taking care of each other and our home, planet Earth. (Economics, Ecology, Ethics and Superposition).

Signposts and insights towards a radical philanthropic [r] evolution; a treatise for remembering our destiny.

In loving memory of Clive Gardiner

No Other Way NOW, Taking Care of Each Other and Our home, planet Earth
© 2022 NOW Who Cares Wins (No Other Way)

David Brook is hereby identified as the author of this work in accordance
with section 77 of the Copyright, Design and Patents Act. 1988. He asserts
and gives notice of his moral right under this Act. The author assigns
Copyright to NOW (No Other Way) C.I.C.

Self-published through KDP Amazon.com.

All proceeds from sale go towards promoting the objectives of the NOW
Movement through NOW (No Other Way) Community Interest Company.

Book Design: Adam Hay Studio

ISBN: 979-8-357-39985-4

Contents

9   **Setting the scene**
15 **Author's note and introduction**
21 **Prologue**
31 **Now's Story**

39 Element One

40 **The Invitation**
43 **Now's raison d'etre, our mission**
47 **Purpose**
49 **Globalisation; the grand delusion**
61 **Evolutionary beings**

75 Element Two

76 **Introduction**
82 **Finite and infinite**
90 **Perfect oneness**
94 **Mind**
96 **Thought, Thinking and Knowledge**

103 Element Three

104 **Memorandum**
107 **Now QED (integral model)**
108 **Introduction and background**
116 **Sustainable Humane Ecology**
123 **SHE Perspectives**
145 **Feminine rising**

151 Element Four

154 **Shared Vision**
156 **Action Research**
157 **Critical Theory**
157 **Dialogue**
159 **Love**

164 **Epilogue**

172 Notes
174 Bibliography and Index

All the world's a stage,
and all the men and
women merely players,
they have their exits
and entrances, and
one man in his time
plays many parts.

WILLIAM SHAKESPEARE

There are no questions,
no answers,
no boundaries,
and no realities…
… that are not of our making or …
… that we have not allowed to be imposed upon us.

It is all of our making.

The future demands that
we work and stand as one.
You are responsible for everything.

Do something about it!

With our thoughts we make the world.

BUDDHA

Setting the scene

Our home planet Earth is under extreme existential threat from the climate crisis, pollution, species extinction, and inequality, all directly caused by the greed of humankind as it colonises and exploits the Earth's scarce, precious, and divine resources. The impact of the climate crisis economically, ecologically, and socially can no longer be denied or tolerated.

Thomas Berry comments: "It has become especially dangerous in Western [now global] culture when our cultural coding has set itself deliberately against our genetic coding and the instinctive tendencies of our genetic endowment are systematically negated. Such is the origin of our present situation.

Our secular, rational, industrial society, with its amazing scientific insight and technological skills, has established the first radically anthropocentric society, and has thereby broken the primary law of the universe: the law of the integrity of the universe. This law states that every component member of the universe should be integral with every other member of the universe and that the primary norm of reality and value is the universe community itself, in its various forms of expression, especially as realised on planet Earth. The new industrial [anthropocentric] coding, which arose in Western society, has now been spread throughout the entire earth."

Deep down we know it's not alright:

The Earth is 4.6 billion years old. Let's scale that to 46 years.

Human beings have been here for 4 hours. Our industrial revolution began 1 minute ago, and in that time, we have destroyed more than 50% of the world's forests. Source: Greenpeace.

Humankind colonises and dominates planet Earth. In 10,000 BC the world population was estimated at 4 million. 11,600 years later in the 16th century it was 500 million. 419 years later in 2019 it was 7.7 billion. Source Ourworlddata.org.

The rapid loss of species we are seeing today is estimated by experts to be between 1,000 and 10,000 times higher than the natural extinction rate. https: wwf.panda.org.

The ice caps are melting, and the world is getting hotter. 19 of the warmest 20 years have all occurred since 2001. Source: NASA global climate changes report.

"We have reached a tipping point. Inequality can no longer be treated as an afterthought. We need to focus the debate on how the benefits of growth are distributed." Angel Gurria OECD Secretary General.

"The 26 richest people held as much wealth as half the global population". Antonio Guterres UN Secretary General.

The top 10.7% of the adult population own 84.1% of the wealth. The bottom 56.6% own 1.8% of the wealth. Source: Credit Suisse global wealth report, 2019.

Whilst we have taken some corrective steps, much of our response to date has been characterised by denial, avoidance and inaction, giving priority to short-term economic, political, and purely anthropocentric considerations. We have much more to do.

Our diverse, socially-constructed cultures and perspectives on reality, rather than being accepted, tolerated, and respected as healthy diversity in humankind's rich tapestry and continuing evolution are increasingly becoming polarised and fragmented as various factions fight for the right to be right (extreme narcissism, always having to be right, forcing your will on others), to be powerful and to dominate increasingly with the use of social media (which is actively used by over a third of the world's population). Social media is heavily populated and polluted by fake news, geopolitical hacking and interference, as well as corporate propaganda challenging all notions of truth and reality, the ramifications of which contribute to ever increasing levels of uncertainty and anxiety.

The world seems to be increasingly dominated by a powerful elite fuelled by corporate, personal, or national monetary greed achieved and sustained through predatory (rather than fair competition) capitalism which is fixated on economic growth and human and ecological exploitation rather than broadening and deepening our understanding of humankind and the contribution we are here to make within the universe. Monetary wealth in the 21st century is absolute power. Any notion of global liberal democracy acting for the common good for all is now but a distant memory, and this must change. The balance between the extreme power of monetary wealth and the indebtedness of democracy to it, must change.

Come, my friends,
'tis not too late to seek
a newer world.

ALFRED LORD TENNYSON

The COVID-19 pandemic then appears early in 2020 as an urgent wake-up call, and within weeks it highlights many deficiencies and raises heartfelt issues associated with inequality, inadequate social care, community, and economy. Within weeks, humanity is in lockdown, with all its dire socio-economic, personal and political consequences. We begin to recognise that both the climate crisis and the COVID-19 pandemic are a result of human behaviour, of our own making.

The world is further shaken in February 2022 by a war within European borders, as President Putin invades the Ukraine and alludes to the potential use of nuclear weapons. NATO and the European Union strengthen their ties and support the Ukraine politically, militarily and financially, as the peace sustained since the end of the Cold War is greatly threatened.

As we grapple with the enormity of it all, much of the rhetoric is calling for a 'new normal'. There is no going back now, only forward, together, as humankind; humans acting kindly, philanthropically and caringly towards all, including the overall ecology of our home, planet Earth. There is no other way to achieve this than through an ever-deeper understanding of what it means to be human, of what it means to love, value, support and learn from each other through peaceful dialogue and from our environment. We must focus on our relationships with each other, the broader ecology of our home, planet Earth, and the cultures, systems and paradigms we create and maintain.

We need to change, and it must be an authentic, real change which can only be achieved through real work and deep learning that changes our DNA. So, where do we begin? As Thomas Berry and Mark Carney say, "We must begin where everything begins, with human affairs", and "A question for every company, every financial institution, every asset manager, pension fund or insurer (a question for everyone) is – what's your plan?"

We appear to have forgotten the ancient wisdom expressed above by the Buddha. Not only our thoughts but also our feelings, actions, perceptions, awareness and experiences make the world we choose; we construct it, but the important word here is choose, as we have total control over how we "make the world". This will become apparent throughout what I have to say herein.

It's

NOW

Or never.

We need to act.
Altogether

NOW

A paradox.

Is all there is and all that we have,
there is no other; I am, that, I am.
No separation. No boundary.

NOW

Because there is No Other Way to
prosper than caring for all our communities,
all their species and their ecology.

NOW

A call to arms.
If you are part of the problem, you need
to become part of the solution.

The

NOW

Hypothesis:

Our essential nature is peace and wholeness.
All mutually arises, is experienced and
known through perfect oneness.
Perfect Oneness determines all.

Tell a wise person or else keep silent, because the mass man will mock it right away, I praise what is truly alive.

JOHAN WOLFGANG VON GOETHE

Author's note and introduction

The quotes on p.14 and p.17 are a good reflection of my condition, of my consciousness (awareness and experience). The first, in so much as I am only interested in deep, meaningful, authentic matters and not at all interested in vacuous and mundane celebrity culture or the media-driven rhetoric associated with much of contemporary life. The second, probably because of the first, reflects the fact that I find it rare that I can talk about my interests, as not many seem to be able to handle such conversations.

Even as a child, this was my reality, resulting in a childhood largely typified as one of not fitting in (along with all the associated fear, stress and trauma that came with it) with what was demanded of me by a dominant, all-powerful cultural paradigm (Roman Catholicism, the UK education system of the 1960s and 1970s, patriarchy and the predatory capitalism and insatiable consumption experienced through the era of Thatcherism) dominated by rules with little or no space for exploration, questioning, curiosity, creativity, wonder, truth-seeking, meaning-seeking or doing good. As I progressed through life, I found it necessary to "kowtow" within this culture to survive. I had to gain acceptance, so I became a cog in the wheel of predatory capitalism and globalisation, and it almost destroyed me.

I later came to realise that you can either accept, or be coerced into, the dominant cultural paradigm (accepted reality) with which you are presented, or you can challenge the status quo. Bettany Hughes speaking of Socrates says: "acquiescence to the status quo [the way things are] is not just lazy, it is inhuman" and "the unexamined life is not worth living" Socrates. Through my reading I came across Plato's concepts of truth-seeking and meaning-seeking as routes to defining authentic reality. Dante's comment from The Divine Comedy "In the middle of the road of my life I awoke in a dark wood where the true way was wholly lost." The insights coming out of the domain of quantum physics concerning whole-ism, along with the other quotations from many other subjects from the sciences and humanities included herein. All of these ideas exactly depicted the substance of my condition and showed me I was not alone. I discovered that my choice was to change the paradigm and my mindset, or to remain in the state that I had been conditioned into by a pathogenic system and culture, "To acquiesce to the status quo".

I have now come to view life as a messy, chaotic, complex web, a deep and continuous learning experience, an education, guided by experience and choice, a creative and emergent process of becoming; a life that, since the time of conception has a unique identity and gifts in formation (and information) to bring forth into the world, a unique contribution to the great unfolding. Above all, life is sacred. Our parents and broader societies need to consciously cultivate and nurture each child as an individual, taking great care not to indoctrinate them, jointly participating with them in learning experiences and sharing the received wisdom (rather than pure dogma), enabling them to "Stand on the shoulders of giants" recognising that "Intuitive knowledge is the highest level of knowledge".[1]

At any point in time, an individual is a product of their experiences, relationship, awareness, thoughts, feelings and choices: the people we encounter, the books we have read, the information we consider, our education, our religion, guided by reflection, inquiry and vision as we formulate our distinct perspective on truth and reality.

Also, before we go much further, I would like to issue a health warning: don't believe in anything I, or the vast array of "giants" that I quote to contribute to our learning experience say, but consider it, inquire into it, let it sit with and wash over you, test it and form your own opinion and then we may indeed advance our understanding.

I've been bringing this together for about eighteen months (after 20 years of engagement with the topics!), sometimes stagnating and at other times flowing. I've always tried to approach it from a state of flow or movement, contributing to it when inspired to do so, rather than systematically, objectively, rationally, thinking it into existence. As with life in general, one is likely to find many paradoxes (as life is complex, messy, chaotic and subjective) contained herein, the first being that I am trying to write down something that ultimately cannot be written about: that which can only be experienced. Reading this is a unique experience from which to hopefully gain a deeper perspective on life; it is, as it were, a stone to ripple the pond, a paradox to ponder, designed

I want to be with those
who know secret things
or else alone.

RILKE

to challenge, provoke and stimulate!

As I was reading and re-reading it through, it took on a life of its own and I find I am ever expanding it, which I suppose is the whole point; it is emergent. However, having reached this staging-post point, I need to clarify what I mean by some of the metaphysical terms to which I have found it difficult to attach definitive, generally accepted meanings:

- Perfect oneness: wholeness, ultimate reality, source, implicit in everything, contains all, knows all, unified field (physics), formless (beyond words and forms), ground of being - God beyond God (Tillich), Brahman, unity, unification; one awareness, collective consciousness, collective unconsciousness (Carl Jung), God, Christ, implicate order (David Bohm), benevolence, all knowing, infinite, unconditional love

- Soul: the manifestation of perfect oneness as reflected through and within all. Also referred to as spirit

- Enlightenment: becoming aware, the realisation of perfect oneness

- Self-consciousness: awareness, experience, mind and thought of individual beings, plants, animals, and things

- Collective consciousness: shared beliefs, ideas, and moral attitudes which can operate as a unifying force at the level of society but also perhaps a deep, underlying, undifferentiated awareness

- Education, learning, growth: the process of moving towards enlightenment

- Ego: self-centred, separate, individual perspective, ignorant of perfect oneness, finite

- The System: consumerism, globalisation, industrialisation, predatory capitalism, fake news, social media, insincere rhetoric, game theory

- Truth: that which does not change.

Soul is a most subjective and emotive word, and as it is frequently used herein and plays an integral part in what I am depicting throughout, I am minded to share James Hillman's insightful take on it:

"To understand the soul, we cannot turn to science. Its best meaning is given by its context... Words associated with soul amplify it further: mind, spirit, heart, life, warmth, humanness, personality, individuality, intentionality, essence, innermost purpose, emotion, quality, virtue, morality, sin, wisdom, death, God.

A soul is said to be troubled, old, disembodied, immortal, lost, innocent, inspired. Eyes are said to be soulless by showing no mercy. The soul has been imaged as... given by God and thus divine, as conscience, as a multiplicity and as a unity in diversity, as a harmony, as a fluid, as fire, as dynamic energy... The search for soul leads always to depths."

There is an acronym known as five W's and H – Who, What, When, Where, Why and How – used as a way of providing information and insight when clarifying a vision, a strategy, knowledge or a problem, and I have loosely tried to depict each of these herein. In Element One I identify the Who and the Why as a way of stating the purpose of the NOW movement. In Element Two I expand on some key aspects of what it means to be human: Self-consciousness, soul, mind, thought, awareness, experience, observation, and action.

In Element Three I utilise many quotations and insights (building on the shoulders of giants) as to the What, which contributes to and further elaborates on and clarifies the Why. Element Four generally focusses on the How; the Where and the When, I hope, should be obvious throughout! However, we should recognise from the outset that it is only this "I" who is separating what is fundamentally whole into these elements. Remember that each element contains the whole, and vice-versa: each element will have a relevance to every other element. An element cannot exist without a context, nor without wholeness.

The content, along with the broader objectives of the NOW (No Other Way) Community Interest Company (see www.nootherway.co.uk) contains the NOW Movement, NOW Academy (learning, education, personal and professional development provider and research forum) and NOW Enterprises (development, facilitation and operation of philanthropic businesses). Each is designed to inquire, challenge, provoke, stimulate, initiate and inspire dialogue in order to evoke positive change and make progress towards our collective enlightenment, moving towards sustainability and reducing inequality for all humans, non-humans and the ecology of our home, planet Earth – and therefore they will cover the whole spectrum of subjects from within the sciences and humanities, both epistemologically and ontologically and beyond. The content of both this book, along with the NOW Movement, foster a transcendent realisation (beyond the normal or physical level) from "This place of terror [separation, insatiable and unsustainable consumerism, dominant predatory capitalism, and all forms of inequality] home to a calm dawn [perfect oneness] and the work we had just begun [the art and practice of love]."[2]

The NOW Academy will draw on an ever-broadening, diverse and sometimes conflicting range of ideas, thoughts, contributors and presenters, to ensure we have the best opportunity of capturing those which make the greatest contribution to achieving both the collective and individual objectives associated with our philosophy, and to avoid becoming dogma. There are likely to be many paths towards these objectives from many varied standpoints and disciplines, so the content as espoused herein (ever to be expanded) is not designed to be definitive and prescriptive, but rather illustrative, challenging, provocative, illuminative, and above all, creative in pursuit of NOW objectives.

NOW represents an awakening process from fragmentation and separation towards wholeness (perfect oneness): the absence of time, the timeless; and the absence of form, the formless; a movement from solely applying logical thought, scientific thinking, reductionism and the conditioning of the forms of our historic creations to fully integrating (making whole) mind, heart and soul to ensure that we do not fall back into patterns of a global culture that have roots in pathological thinking and have brought us to face our own extinction.

The content herein are factors, forces, philosophies, scientific understandings, psychological and sociological theories, etc, coupled with the many quotations that have together had the greatest impact on my life so far and appear to present the best opportunities to overcome the existential challenges we are facing, and they will be a bellwether in determining people's interest to join and participate in the NOW Family. It would not have been possible for me to write this without their inspiration, they have been instrumental and formational in my personal learning experience and towards the development of NOW. I thank them unreservedly and strongly recommend that you explore their work further.

I am aware that some of what follows could be viewed as a polemic: a passionate argument, and a little idiosyncratic, individual, and distinctive; and so, it is. It is a passionate and individual argument, and it reflects my interpretation of the world that I am experiencing, but as Bohm once said, "All that can ever really be said is this is how it appears to one at this point in time, but one has no way of truly knowing that in the next second, minute, hour, week, month, year... that some new information won't be found and everything you previously had thought changes."

So, this is how it appears to me, now.

Prologue

HUMAN ARISING

Towards an emergent creation theory, (that unknown element, see Arthur Schopenhauer contingency and anthropic principle p.47 and Barrow/Tippler p.132) not a belief, one of infinite designed intelligence forever emerging and unfolding.

It is amazing that we exist at all.

Let us reflect for a moment on what brings perfect oneness manifesting as soul into the human form, from the formless into a world of forms, from the infinite to the finite and ultimately back to the formless and infinite, where in fact, forms and finitude are merely expressions of the same underlying, unbounded formless and infinite as presented herein. I postulate that it is the human mind that is creating the illusion of finite forms, of separateness, which is the root cause of all our problems and challenges, and we need to address the root not the symptoms.

We are called into this world through what is one of the most complex life-producing biological processes. From a purely separate materialist perspective some may say – as from this perspective they lack factual material evidence of how life and consciousness (the "hard" problems) arise – that it is the most magical, mystical, or miraculous process known to humankind, and because they can't find how it arises through their reductionist, objective approaches, they simply choose to ignore it. However, for me it is simply what is: awareness, perfect oneness, whole. After millions of cell divisions, the foetus is created. A new-born baby has 26 billion cells and it is estimated that there are 100 trillion atoms per cell, which rises to 50 trillion cells in an adult. At which point is it human (indeed the classification "human" is created by humans)? At every point since conception. When is the soul present? Always. Human

21

birth (along with all the innate creative potential that surrounds us always, everywhere) is a spectacular event by any measure of science or spirituality. From a mathematical perspective, it is estimated that the chances of you being born as you are 1 in 4 trillion – you are that lucky to be here, so make your life extraordinary.

From the moment of conception, the baby has started on an incredible journey of arising in the world, becoming manifest, something we classify as "self", (but something that never separates from perfect oneness) within the ground of being. There is however a bigger process of evolution to which becoming human belongs, that inter-connection with everything. We have in the truest sense evolved from stardust, as carbon is only formed in stars and it is the second most abundant element in the human body; without it, we would not exist. We are the conscious reflection and explicit manifestation of what Bohm calls implicate order, what Eastern Indian mystics call sutra (thread or string), what many religions call God, what the Red Indians call The Great Spirit, what quantum mechanics call the unified field, what I refer to here as perfect oneness. There is a strand that connects all things; it is from where we have come: our source. It is what we are, and it is to where we will inevitably return. It is a dimension beyond the time and space that are merely human constructs. This is true creationism; all relating, constantly and infinitely creating form from formlessness and then back to formlessness again, finite from infinite and then back to infinite, the whole perfect oneness in creation.

John O'Donohue in *Divine Beauty; The Invisible Embrace*, comments:

"There is no other way into the world except through the body of a woman. Woman is the portal to the universe. She is also the womb of *being*. Each person in the world commenced life as a miniscule trace within depths of the mother whose womb is the space where that trace expands and opens to assume human form. In terms of one's later identity and destiny abroad in the world, this is the time for ultimate formation and influence.

In human encounters, there is nothing nearer to this; no two humans ever come closer than when one is forming in the other's depths. Naturally the relationship is hugely imbalanced: the one is a complete person; the other is miniscule and is just beginning a journey towards identity through absorbing life from the mother.

No man ever comes nearer a woman, no woman ever comes nearer to a woman. This intricate nurturing into identity takes place below the light in the physical sub consciousness of her body. The whole journey is a hidden one. It is the longest human journey from the invisible to the visible. From every inner pathway, the labyrinth of her body brings a flow of life to form and free this inner pilgrim. Imagine the incredible events that are coming to form within the embryo: how each particle of growth is like the formation of a world from fragments."

The human life force, indeed, the whole of life, the birthing of everything coming forth, creation, is born of feminine energy[3], so it is not surprising to find even the cutting edge of science, quantum physics, pulling towards this feminine energy: "An object with billions of stars like the milky way began life as a quantum fluctuation (similar to "minuscule trace" above). It now appears as if the quantum world has shaped everything. Something that was a tiny fluctuation becomes our galaxy in a cluster of galaxies."[4] This tiny mysterious fluctuation is metaphoric of the miniscule trace of the first cell division in a human fertilised egg. Seemingly from nothing life emerges.

I have been inspired by many pop songs over the years. Often the lyrics can get drowned out somewhat by the music. A particular and relevant favourite of mine which provides a uniquely powerful message and metaphor for our current circumstances and resonates well with the content herein is by The Waterboys and I would love to have included its full lyrics here. Its lyrics are set to dramatic music which invokes a sense of urgency – it is revolutionary. It is full of poetic rhythm, and metaphor. It could easily be described as NOW's rallying call – it inspires.

However due to copyright law I am not easily permitted to reproduce the full lyrics here even though they are freely available on several sites on the internet and therefore, somewhat arcanely in respect of openness and creative application, I have to direct you to: https://www.lyrics.com/lyric/4619318/Various+Artists/Don%27t+Bang+the+Drum and https://www.youtube.com/watch?v=GMe3jdhXA3E. Please do not read further until you have read the lyrics and listened to the song.

The relevance for us here is that we find ourselves on a remarkably fertile, living, naturally self-sustaining (where it not for humankinds recent behaviour) planet, engaging with the vibrational energy that is life. We are here for a soulful experience and purpose, to find and apply for the benefit of all our gifts and to make them manifest.

For me, the song raises my energy and excites me, invoking a spiritual connection with all: our home, planet Earth, our ancestors, with our spiritual nature and with our bodies, challenging us to open our minds to dream, to imagine and to envision a better world through a natural and eternal flow, and represents a call to action. What are you going to do? How will you act? Will you just repeat history or learn from it not to keep making the same mistakes? Will you just "acquiesce to the status quo"? It also directly and urgently challenges us to make a unique contribution to the everlasting cosmic unfolding as opposed to the status quo of globalisation, and to the ecological destruction of the divine ground upon which we stand, ground that we have deemed profane, not worthy of respect and less important than the fulfilment of our wants. Don't let the unique contribution you are here to make pass you by through just following the heard. We will not have that here, no more, not in our name.

Will you stand with us in this special, fabulous NOW place? And:

If not you, who?
If not here, where?
If not now, when?

The majority of our lives are either socially constructed (e.g., economics, religion, globalisation etc.) or physically constructed in support of our social constructions and these would not exist if we did not manifest and sustain them; we metaphorically bring forth what we determine to be reality.

As I will seek to demonstrate, even leading physicists and scientists are now joining many psychologists, philosophers and theologians, pointing to the impact of conscious will in determining physical world entities. We know we do this at a tangible, physical level: we create material things by combining chemicals, minerals and other elements, but they are also demonstrating the importance and fundamental role of the observer, of conscious agents[5] making a measurement, and as far as we know humans are the most advanced life form doing such, in determining reality at the energetic, subatomic level: the collapse of wave function. We are indeed true alchemists.

So, we have 7.5 billion unique human beings, each with an individual perspective on our constructions of what we take to be reality (realities), some of which we share and resonate with others as we group together in various cultures and sub-cultures, and whilst these can provide cohesion, they can also cause, or be used for conflict, derision, confusion and damage as we "fight for the right to be right", rather than holding the space for understanding and enlightenment to emerge, rather than being valued for their contribution to a richer, deeper, picture and understanding of our realities, thereby making us more humane, moral and right-minded.

Clearly our constructions, our realities, are of our creation. They are projections of our morals, values, wishes, ideals, imagination, beliefs, needs, wants and egos (that which separates), and they are not an absolute, pre-ordained, purely objective reality existing "out there" separately from us as we or others may like us to think. Our realities are an ethereal, fluid, emerging and creative phenomenon mutually arising in perfect oneness. They are the realities we chose to create and maintain, and therefore, no matter how complex or intransigent the resulting problems may appear, they can be changed in an instant if we so wish, such changes being generally referred to as paradigm shifts. The future can only result from our imagination. Indeed, the past, present and future all arise through our memory, perception and imagination.

NOW is forming a community and a holding space from which such shifts can emerge and evolve. The initial challenge taken up by NOW is to recognise, realise and utilise (for the benefit of all) what rests behind, what is fundamental to our constructions and the current deterministic, materialistic scientific-dominant worldview. What is it that is constructing, why has it been constructed to these current ends, is this what was intended, and is this the best we can do?

What rests behind is what we call herein perfect oneness, it is everywhere, always, and never fully separated.

'Who we are' and 'why we are here' questions have challenged many great thinkers throughout the millennia including scientists, philosophers, psychologists, theologians etc, but not so much, I suspect, at least not in the application of their professions, by those in politics, business, commerce and economics (mainly market based activities) who generally practice their professions by very tight, clearly defined rules and boundaries as represented through globalisation – otherwise we would not be facing the current existential challenges that we are.

Globalisation has provided many benefits and contributed greatly to improving socio-economic wellbeing when compared to the proceeding centuries, however its current use and application has reached its limit and it is no longer "fit for purpose", especially considering the ramifications of Russia's invasion of the Ukraine (insecure global energy supplies, a huge rise in inflation and unstable essential food supplies), and therefore needs to evolve radically if humanity is to thrive rather than become extinct. It is these later professions (see above) that can help build a new business logic based on the NOW philosophy through a spirit of transformation in order to create a more sustainable and radically philanthropic model, once they have considered these questions and moved beyond the narrow confines of their tightly rule-bound professions and cultures, once their consciousness, knowledge and understanding expand and evolve to a higher plane.

Clearly, market-based activities are embedded in market-based assumptions and economic rules, which, in summary are commonly reflected by the adage "all other things being equal" (provided that other factors or circumstances remain the same) along with the application of Laissez-Faire economics (an economic doctrine that opposes governmental regulation of or interference in commerce beyond the minimum necessary for a free-enterprise system to operate according to its own economic laws). Both of these, I would suggest, realistically are rarely or ever the case, so they could be a false assumption, based on outdated social constructs.

Indeed, the serious matters in life cannot be calculated; that's why economics ignores them. By way of example, I once walked over a disused

Imagination is the hotline into meaning.

LINDSAY CLARKE

coal mine in South Wales (Fernhill) with a prominent mining engineer who had spent all his working life in coal mining. At Fernhill, the waste material that's dug out to get to the coal (which to this day still covers much of the South Wales Valleys) covered the whole site of over 200 acres, to a depth of tens of meters, and it still smelt strongly of coal, where wire cables and iron from old railway tracks protruded from the ground. I asked the engineer "didn't anyone think about the ecological damage and scarring of the landscape or what the potential alternatives might be?" and he said that some did. One answer to the problem was to put the waste material back from whence it came, underground, which seemed very logical so I asked why they didn't do it and he said it would have made the whole process uneconomic! This is by no means an isolated event. Indeed, I would argue that much economic activity is only profitable, or profitable to the extent demanded by the capital markets, if one chooses to ignore the full costs associated with such activity.

This capacity or choice of ignoring or lacking adequate foresight of "other factors" (subjective) which don't fit the prevailing dominant paradigm could be argued to have been at the centre of the propaganda campaign by the oil industry of the late '80s and early '90s against the clear evidence of global warming, the disastrous financial collapses of the past few decades, and trusting that President Putin was aligned with a global peaceful paradigm, along with others. There is also perhaps a similarity with "all other things being equal" (in so much that it contends that no other elements change or that we are not aware of them), identified by physicists, hypothetically, as "dark matter/energy", which accounts for circa 85% of the universe, and of which they have little understanding, but which is probably having some form of impact, and it would be foolish to ignore it.

Economics, ethics, politics, theology, philosophy, psychology and science are all social (human) constructs or manifestations. Let's take science for example, but there are similar examples from the humanities as well. Science likes to think it is founded upon empirical, objective observation, prediction and repeatability, but as quantum physicists delve further into what they thought was solid observable matter they find that atoms are far from solid or predictable (Heisenberg's uncertainty principle[6]) and are in fact made up of fluctuating quanta. Every time scientists think they have found the ultimate quanta (fermions, leptons, quarks, bosons, gluons, strings...) something else emerges, and even the act of observance changes or perhaps determines (creates) the result, the reality. Perhaps even the observer is creating the ever-emerging new quanta and will always do so. Such a paradigm questions whether anything can be labelled as purely objective or whether we can ever know anything objectively as separate entities from the things we observe as we are always determining (affecting) it. Indeed the "it" does not exist apart from our interaction and interpretation with "it", "it" is always "us" (I am that I am, Exodus 3:14). I am therefore: everything, everywhere, always now, forever, awareness, feeling and experience. Perhaps it truly is better not to spend all the billions of pounds spent on the LHC (large hadron collider) seeking the ultimate particles as they don't exist apart from our bringing them into form and we should spend that money more wisely.

NOW is both a paradox and a contradiction. It is a paradox because the now (present) is all we ever experience but generally we take it to be but a fleeting moment. It is a contradiction in so much as whilst we may generally accept that there is only *now,* the ever-present present, that which we can only ever experience, you can't directly experience the future or the past; the future is a constructed, selected vision of our imagination and the past is a constructed, selected memory; we generally spend the "now" mainly commenting on the past or forecasting the future.

Perhaps we are scared to know what we truly are and don't want to know what rests behind and creates our social constructions and the broader questions posed here because it would challenge current power bases, because the answer is just so incredible and runs so counter to the beliefs currently maintained by the modernist scientific dominant paradigm and powerful elites. Because we are so awesome, fantastic and creators and perceivers of all that we take to be reality, it is insane for us to act and interact as we do, assuming that reality exists "out there" apart from me, us, everything, and that we can do nothing about it. There really is no separation and we can do everything about it.

NOW, because there really is no other way than recognising that there are an infinite number of ways and we get to determine them; and in recognising the infinite we are recognising perfect oneness, we come to know who we truly are... we get to choose.

The universe is
made of stories
not of atoms.

MURIEL RUKEYSER

Now's Story

As Thomas Berry says in his book *The Dream of the Earth* "It's all a question of story": the stories we tell ourselves, the stories we tell others, the stories we are told, and coupled with our social constructs, our lives are a mix of evolving stories. We are storytellers.

Stories are how we frame, portray and project our individual and collective meanings, beliefs, realities, awareness's and experiences. They are the narrative by which we define our past, present and future, all from within the ever-present now. They are how we communicate, and there are many ways they can be told. As stories they are imbued with myth, legend, fact, fiction, drama, hopes, dreams, visions and fear, the whole gamut of life. There is both an art and a science to storytelling, and authentic storytelling is both a key attribute and skill supporting human existence as an important element in the cosmos, its great unfolding, its evolution and emergence.

Berry goes on to say we are in trouble right now, a crisis of storytelling: "We are in between stories. The old story, the account of how the world came to be and how we fit into it, is no longer effective. Yet we have not learned the new story. Presently this traditional story is dysfunctional.... even with advanced science and technology, with superb techniques in manufacturing, in communications and computations [our current dominant story] our secular society remains without satisfactory meaning or social discipline needed for a life leading to emotional, aesthetic, and spiritual fulfilment." The dysfunction Berry mentions is represented in our continuing destruction of our home, planet Earth, along with all the species (including humans) that rely upon her for their existence and nourishment. Our global society is mainly driven by greed, over-consumption, separateness, wars, and an egotistic mindset. Such dysfunction, its propaganda and resulting news is then propagated either truthfully or "fake" by social media, along with the resulting globalised story

31

proffered seeks to condition the population for its own ends, and – let's be clear about this – they are not choosing such through some ethically robust transparent open-source democracy or market-based system that cares for their and the planet's wellbeing.

Such dysfunction is being continually indoctrinated in our dominant cultures, whether purposefully by the powerful, wealthy elites (popularly known as the 1%'ers) or systemised into our way of being as we maintain cultures rooted in past mistakes. This is what inhibits and supresses our authentic human story from being told, shared, practiced, and further unfolded. When convenient, please watch "The Social Dilemma" on Netflix for further useful insights on surveillance capitalism.

"In 1928 the richest 1% could expect to capture around 15% of the wealth, of the income. In 2018 the same 1% got more than 85% of the entire money generated across Europe."[7] It is practically impossible to do anything without money in our current culture, and so what the foregoing quote is pointing to is that in 1928 99% of the population had 85% of the wealth from which to realise their creative/entrepreneurial potential, but by 2018, this had reduced to 99% of the population having 15% of the wealth thereby increasing inequality in this respect. This was also heavily influenced by the consolidation of the power by the elites fuelled by the Industrial Revolution, the technological/ industrial revolution, and the growth of predatory capitalism.

Steve Bannon has an interesting view following the financial crash in 2007/8: "This is what upsets me about the lack of accountability and responsibility by the world's elites, we just went through the worst financial crisis in history. Not one CEO went to jail and not anybody significantly gave up any equity. What they did fundamentally was to inflate. On 18 Sept 2008[8] the balance sheet of the Federal Reserve was $880 billion. On 20 Jan 2017 it was $4.5 trillion. All we did in the Bank of England, European Central Bank, Bank of Japan (et al) was to save the elites. They turned on the sprinklers of liquidity so that if you owned assets – real estate, stock, or IP – you've had the greatest 10-year run in history. If you are working-class schmendricks, your wages are flat. It is reckless disregard what the elites have done."

This represents well many political actions in respect of the application and management of predatory capitalism and globalisation, whereby profits and benefits are privatised (for the protection of directors and shareholders), and losses are socialised (spread over the general population).

Colin Murphy a BBC presenter asks[9], "Why are the rich allowed to ruin our planet? From 1990-2015, that's a critical period in which our annual emissions grew 60% and cumulative emissions doubled. The richest 10% of the world's population were responsible for 52% of the cumulative number. The poorest 50% of the population – 3.1 billion people – produced just 7% of emissions;

they used just 4% of the available carbon budget as it's called. The richest 1% is just 63 million people and they were solely responsible for 15% and 9% of the carbon budget.

Since 2015, there have been changes of course, but not nearly enough, and if you think enough has changed then consider the fact that just 100 companies globally are the source for more than 70% of greenhouse gas emissions since 1988[10]. So just let that sink in.

How many adverts or campaigns have you seen aimed at big industry when it comes to the climate crisis and how many have you seen aimed at the poorest 50% about the right thing to buy to cut down the personal carbon footprint and to use certain shopping bags? Yet here's the facts: we can all be positively angelic and that will not be enough because it's actually big business and the very richest (despite having the means to make the biggest changes) that are still causing most of the problem. Now does that mean we should all just stop? No, of course not. We all have a roll, we can all try and do better, but why is most public awareness about buying bags for life and cutting down our individual footprint when the biggest offenders are the rich?"

Perfect oneness is aware that it contains some who are tormented souls (those who only see separateness) and some who have elements of themselves that are tormented: they are either too blind, too ignorant, too self-centred, too traumatised, fearful and or too arrogant to recognise the divine in all things, of which they are an element. They are either unaware of or in fear of their divine nature. These tormented souls create and maintain power through illusions designed to exploit and impoverish the masses, and as such they keep themselves and those they enslave in the darkness.

The preceding paragraphs of this section and some of what follows depict a society that has lost its way. There is a poem by David Wagoner called "Lost", which was introduced to me by a poet called David Whyte, one which I have recited many times in many workshops, one that has a particular relevance here, as it deals with what you should do when you are lost:

LOST

Stand still.
The trees ahead and bushes beside you
Are not lost.
Wherever you are is called Here,
And you must treat it as a powerful stranger,
Must ask permission to know it and be known.
The forest breathes.
Listen. It answers
I have made this place around you,
If you leave it you may come back again, saying Here.
No two trees are the same to Raven.
No two branches are the same to Wren.
If what a tree or a bush does is lost on you,
You are surely lost.
Stand still.
The forest knows
Where you are. You must let it find you.

I commend this poem to you and urge you to read it out loud, along with all the other poems and quotes referenced herein, so you can hear your own voice and make them come alive. I also urge you to recite them often, as some deeper insight always emerges. Whilst the poem clearly has its own message, I would like to share with you the relevance I see for it here.

STAND STILL

There is a tendency when we feel lost to rush around frantically looking for the answers or doing more of the same, only harder, and then we "can't see the wood for the trees", we can't hear the messages coming from our environment and we increase our stress levels when in fact we should slow down, stand still and listen.

THE TREES AHEAD AND BUSHES BESIDE YOU ARE NOT LOST

It is our perception of our context that is lost and dissonant. We can draw great comfort from those natural things around us that have no concept of being "lost" and we can receive the blessing of contentment in their being – therefore we can learn from them, from the messages they have for us and draw great strength from them.

WHEREVER YOU ARE IS CALLED HERE, AND YOU MUST TREAT IT AS A POWERFUL STRANGER, MUST ASK PERMISSION TO KNOW IT AND BE KNOWN.

We can only ever experience "here" (and I cover this more in depth later) and obviously we each carry around with us our own individual perceptions of "here". This "here" is our own individual perspective on all that we have chosen to accept as our reality, which results from our education, experiences, actions, and relationships. You know what it is like to be in the presence of an imminent threat ("powerful stranger"). You freeze like a cat when it raises its fur and arches its back in the presence of an aggressive dog, or a rabbit frozen in a car's headlight. During these times we must quickly and critically assess the situation from deep within our authentic selves, be present, have heightened awareness and assess or "know" the situation through an intuitive information exchange and quick learning.

THE FOREST BREATHES.

There is always a much bigger context (the metaphoric forest), especially within the natural environment of which we are an integral element – and its breathing (the etymology of the word "spirit" comes from breath) has a calming effect and puts matters in perspective.

LISTEN.

Listening along with stillness is key, but generally we tend to fill the space for listening with noise and distraction because of the perceived urgency of our situation.

IT ANSWERS

The "forest", both actually and metaphorically, is a living system full of ancient wisdom, and if we listen through the stillness within the womb of her being, the answers will arrive.

I HAVE MADE THIS PLACE AROUND YOU.

You are always part of a larger context, an integral part of nature. All our problems and challenges arise from humankind seeing itself as separate; apart from nature.

IF YOU LEAVE IT YOU MAY
COME BACK AGAIN, SAYING HERE.

Once we accept ourselves as a reflection of nature, as part of the forest, of being here and whole, whenever we erroneously separate ourselves, we know we can always return.

NO TWO TREES ARE THE SAME TO RAVEN.
NO TWO BRANCHES ARE THE SAME TO WREN.

This represents our union through diversity.

IF WHAT A TREE OR A BUSH DOES IS LOST
ON YOU, YOU ARE SURELY LOST.

We will remain lost until we accept ourselves as not separate from our circumstances but the cause of them. Once we recognise ourselves as elemental with the "forest", we cannot be lost.

STAND STILL.
THE FOREST KNOWSWHERE YOU ARE.
YOU MUST LET IT FIND YOU.

Says it all.

As Berry says, we need to "educate, heal, guide and discipline. We must begin where everything begins with human affairs - with the basic story, our narrative of how things came to be as they are, and how the future can be given some satisfying direction" a direction founded upon sustainability, and philanthropy a story founded upon authenticity, a story as a natural fundamental element of the greater whole.

This new story must be guided by virtues if we are to achieve futures worthy of our species. These are well identified by Alexander Gesswein as: "profound honesty, courage, curiosity, scepticism, reason, health, discipline, creativity, openness, compassion, fortitude, understanding, imagination, tolerance, patience, laughter, friendship and self-love", to which I would add empathy. For NOW this is the beginning of our construction of our new story (ies) and our new reality (ies).

Before reading further please watch this video by Jeff Lieberman: www.youtube.com/watch?v=N0--_R6xThs.

In ignorance
I am something.
In understanding
I am nothing.
In love
I am everything.

RUPERT SPIRA

ELEMENT ONE

Who are we, what
are we doing and
**why we are we
doing it?**

The Invitation

It doesn't interest me what you do for a living.
I want to know what you ache for
and if you dare to dream of meeting your heart's longing.

It doesn't interest me how old you are.
I want to know if you will risk looking like a fool
for love
for your dream
for the adventure of being alive.

It doesn't interest me what planets are squaring your moon.
I want to know if you have touched the centre of your own sorrow
if you have been opened by life's betrayals
or have become shrivelled and closed
from fear of further pain.

I want to know if you can sit with pain
mine or your own
without moving to hide it
or fade it
or fix it.

I want to know if you can be with joy
mine or your own
if you can dance with wildness
and let the ecstasy fill you to the tips of your fingers and toes
without cautioning us
to be careful
to be realistic
to remember the limitations of being human.

It doesn't interest me if the story you are telling me
is true.
I want to know if you can
disappoint another
to be true to yourself.
If you can bear the accusation of betrayal

and not betray your own soul.
If you can be faithless
and therefore trustworthy.

I want to know if you can see Beauty
even when it is not pretty
every day.
And if you can source your own life
from its presence.

I want to know if you can live with failure
yours and mine
and still stand at the edge of the lake
and shout to the silver of the full moon,
"Yes."

It doesn't interest me
to know where you live or how much money you have.
I want to know if you can get up
after the night of grief and despair
weary and bruised to the bone
and do what needs to be done
to feed the children.

It doesn't interest me who you know
or how you came to be here.
I want to know if you will stand
in the centre of the fire
with me
and not shrink back.

It doesn't interest me where or what or with whom
you have studied.
I want to know what sustains you
from the inside
when all else falls away.

I want to know if you can be alone
with yourself
and if you truly like the company you keep
in the empty moments.

Oriah, *Mountain Dreamer*

No Other Way

COMMUNITY INTEREST COMPANY

Promoting, innovating and delivering social, economic and ecological sustainability through philanthropic and ethical enterprise, education, learning and development.

A Movement for a sustainable, humane world
A Movement for ecovisionary" leadership
A Movement based on stewardship
A Movement of enterprise, creativity, and innovation
A Movement for tomorrow, today, NOW.

Anyone can become rich, powerful, and dominant by destroying our planet and impoverishing the majority of its population.

It takes someone special to rise to great challenges, to save the world and prosper at the same time.

If that someone special could be you, you are in the right place because, you and I together are one.

Everything happens for a reason.

Now's raison d'etre, our mission

The pursuit of ever-deeper awareness, experience, understanding, knowledge and enlightenment, through the questioning of certainties, cultivation of an inquiring mind, challenging taken-for-granted assumptions and thus the expansion of the role and contribution of humanity to the wellbeing of an emerging universe.

We do this by deploying Radical Philanthropy (doing good) and Disruptive Innovation (transforming markets) through Integral Human Development (ecological, personal, and social) in order to overcome humankind's negative impact on our home, planet Earth; reduce inequality and improve wellbeing for all life.

Our motto is: to transform rather than transcend life; to strive, to serve, to love, to learn.

Our mission lies at the heart of all we do, working through a model that continuously improves ecological, social and economic wellbeing, and more equitably distributes ownership and the profit created. It is not just a place or a method but a representation of a way of being, not just about business but about how we choose to live our lives. All NOW companies will be constituted as Community Interest Companies and therefore not for private gain. The NOW model will seek to limit the corrosive impact of capitalism by being:

- Aligned with the United Nations' 17 sustainable development goals to transform our world. (See UN.org).

- Committed to enabling philanthropic social and ecological enterprises: organisations and businesses that are set up to change the world from the inside out. Like traditional businesses we aim to make a profit, but it's what we do with our profits that sets us apart – reinvesting or donating them to create positive social or ecological change.

- Dedicated to maximising Blue Economy principles and practices wherever possible, using the resources available in cascading systems – where the waste of one product becomes the input to create a new cashflow wherever possible.

- Pay the money we use its rightful return: an interest appropriate to the risk of the project through loans secured on trade and business assets or equity.

- Committed to applying an ideology which advances altruistic mindfulness relating with all: each other, the non-human world, and our home, planet Earth.

In doing so:

- We seek to maximise revenue through providing high-quality products and services at competitive market rates.

- We apply prudence to limit any negative impact on the environment, and where possible, we aim to actively enhance it.

- We seek to source all materials and services from within a fifty-mile radius of the major business activity, increasing the distance only where necessary. We also aim to apply "mixed economy"[12] principles to ensure vibrant, dynamic, and above all healthy, sustainable, local and broader economies.

- We seek to raise social standards by paying upper-quartile market rates of pay, and to utilise unemployed staff wherever practicable.

- Where local businesses do not exist to fulfil our needs, we will seek to support their creation where appropriate.

- A minimum of 65% of profits will be either retained within each C.I.C. or used or donated to improve social wellbeing and ecological sustainability.

- A percentage of equity, depending on each individual enterprise, will be owned by owner-operators through partners' mutual trusts.

Where am I going?
What am I doing?
What is the meaning of life?

Whatever is good
for your soul... do that

ANONYMOUS.

Purpose

We start with purpose and meaning. Purpose is the reason something is done or created, and meaning is the message being conveyed, breakthrough or release. Philosophers have pondered the purpose and meaning of life for centuries. For Schopenhauer, "Those who don't wonder about the contingency of their existence, of the contingency of the world's existence, are mentally deficient." I'm glad to say, at least by this definition, I'm not mentally deficient! Perhaps we need to probe a little deeper into what is meant by the argument supporting the "contingency of existence" (otherwise called the Anthropic Principle [13]). The proposition goes something like this: everything around us – including ourselves, the stars and planets – could have failed to exist, and had it not existed, the universe would not exist and so is contingent. Consequently, there must therefore be some reason it does exist, whatever that may be (also see Barrow/Tipler quote on p.132).

As mentioned previously, this work represents a staging post, a work-in-progress, a culmination-to-date of thoughts, experiences, insights, visions, feelings, emotions, hopes and concerns that I seem to share with those who have had similar experiences and are on similar paths, wondering about the "contingency of existence": Jiddu Krishnamurti, Bohm, Albert Einstein, Leo Tolstoy, Dante, Carl Jung, Thomas Kuhn, Rudolf Steiner, Max Horkheimer, Sigmund Freud, Socrates, Fritz Schumacher, Rupert Spira and Jonathan Stedall, to name but a few, and many more less well known but nonetheless insightful thinkers.

The content herein is initially being developed within the NOW (No Other Way) C.I.C. before going on to be further developed with others, the NOW Movement. The content will become the basis for the NOW Academy and for other forms of education, learning, development and NOW Enterprises. It identifies what I consider to be the main causes, both epistemological and ontological, of the critical challenges we face as human beings. These challenges have the potential to destroy humankind and all the other inhabitants of our home, planet Earth. However, through our capacity for imaginative thought, creativity, compassion, humility, and our ability to learn, we have the capacity to correct our errors, change our behaviour and avoid disaster.

Globalisation; the grand delusion

"The Earth provides enough to satisfy everyone's needs but not for everyone's greed."

GANDHI

Deep down we know it's not alright. The ice is melting.

"Anyone who believes in indefinite growth on a finite planet is either mad or an economist."

SIR DAVID ATTENBOROUGH

In Western culture, the primary focus is on the individual self, generally referred to and represented by the ego, with the rights and duties of such individuals forming the bedrock of its laws. Christopher Lasch identifies with the "minimal self", wherein he recognises the tendency for increasing narcissism, with a defensive core.... "Self-centred, self-obsessed with ego gratification, social status, and the pursuit of hedonic pleasure". The focus on self separates the human being from all that is around them, and there is a tendency for anything which is not perceived as the self to be in competition with or under threat from it. This minimal (separate) self then acts against all that it does not perceive as itself. This anthropocentric, separate way of looking at our environment (by environment I mean everything and anything we are aware of: material things, energy, fields, thoughts, feelings or emotions along with the stories we tell and the cultures we inhabit) is the root cause of most of our challenges. We have created the problems, and our ability to create and determine reality is our only chance to solve them.

Quantum physicists, biologists and ecologists would generally agree that human beings are part of an integrated whole, where everything impacts everything else, however this would be anathema to the isolationist minimal self that we have created. Warwick Fox says we should be wary of this anthropocentric view of reality "Because anthropocentric assumptions that magnify our sense of self-importance in the larger scheme of things are obviously self-serving assumptions." He gives a clear example "when was the last time we tried to convince our employer that they were paying us too much...". He refers to these as "truths of convenience".

Issues associated with the minimal self are endemic throughout our dominant global culture and reveal themselves through power, greed and dominance framed within an ever-increasing bureaucratic and panoptical setting compounded and encouraged through social technology and social media which seeks to further support and encourage the concept of the minimal self and to exploit it purely for the benefit of their owners and investors – who themselves epitomise the minimal self (also see reference to Edward Bernays below). The resulting dominant culture is one where individuals and non-dominant cultural groups compete rather than cooperate, seeking to maximise their dominance and power in order to self-actualise and impose their view of reality as the only conceivable way.

In the 1920s, Bernays, a nephew of Freud, introduced the concept of the psychology and propaganda of consumerism, whereby through understanding what motivated people you could influence their behaviour – without them knowing about it. Bernays is quoted in 1928 as saying "In almost every act of our daily lives we are dominated by the relatively small number of persons that understand the mental processes of the masses. It is they that pull the wires which control the public mind". In today's world those "Pulling the wires [the "wires" being mainly computer code algorithms] which control the public mind" are predominantly the social media, technology and general media giants and moguls: Facebook, Google, Twitter, Fox News, Apple, global finance, global corporations and others, as depicted in "The Social Dilemma".[14]

In the 1950s, many of Bernays' ideas, coupled with the use of propaganda and subliminal advertising, were encapsulated in game theory: a systemised model of competitive, strategic interaction between rational decision-makers acting selfishly (minimal selves) and such attributes have been increasingly applied in economics, politics and sociology, and have become the norm as one is conditioned into a systemised routine. According to game theory, every action – good or bad – can be rationalized in the name of self-interest. Critiques of game theory include that human behaviour is frequently irrational, unselfish and cooperative, however, to quote Bernays again, there are a "Relatively small number of persons pulling the wires that control the public mind" through rhetoric and propaganda.

This concept and theory set in place the notion of ever-increasing consumption with the associated, ever-increasing supply and need for ever-increasing capital, and so the stage was set for some disastrous unintended (perhaps!) consequences.

The advent of "fake news" delivered through privately-owned, global social-media and news corporations such as FOX News and Twitter are seen by many to have greatly influenced and enabled BREXIT and the election of Donald Trump as President of the United States, amongst other things, as they seek to control and influence the masses for their own ends, having built upon Bernays' ideas. It is estimated that Americans are exposed to between 4,000 and 10,000 adverts each day,[15] leaving one wondering what is "real" and what is being spun in order to coerce us into mass subjugation, either intentionally or unintentionally, by governments, corporations and individuals – or indeed by the technology itself. For a deeper insight into the propaganda of consumerism and media control, when convenient please watch https://www.youtube.com/watch?v=8l5fRI-YnGo.

Much of the foregoing is eloquently illuminated and predicted by Alexis de Tocqueville in *Democracy in America*, published in 1831:

"I seek to trace the novel features under which despotism may appear in the world. The first that strikes the observation is an innumerable multitude of men, all equal and alike, incessantly endeavouring to procure the petty and paltry pleasures with which they glut their lives. Each of them, living apart, is a stranger to the fate of all the rest; his children and his private friends constitute to him the whole of mankind. As for the rest of his fellow citizens, he is close to them, but he does not see them; he touches them, but he does not feel them; he only exists in himself and himself alone... Above this race of men stands an immense tutelary power, which takes upon itself alone to secure their gratifications and to watch over their fate. That power is absolute, minute, regular, provident, and mild. It would be like the authority of a parent if, like that authority, its object was to prepare men for manhood; but it seeks, on the contrary, to keep them in perpetual childhood; it is well content that the people should rejoice, provided they think of nothing but rejoicing."

An example of the most recent application of the above is the technological, information, and social-media revolution, which is utilising the foregoing for its own ends. As Thomas Friedman points out:[16]

"What's globalising the world and knitting it together is digital technology through on-line courses, through PayPal, through Facebook, through Twitter etc. We are in the middle of three giant hockey stick [graph depiction] accelerators in the market [globalisation], Mother Nature [the climate crisis] and technology [Moore's law[17]] and they are not just changing your world; they are reshaping your world and they are reshaping five realms: politics, geo-politics, the workplace, ethics, and community.

What the hell happened in 2007 – what the hell happened in 2007! Here's what happened in 2007: Steve Jobs introduced the first iPhone – a handheld computer with more computing power in it than the Apollo space mission – Facebook opened its platform to anyone with an email address, Facebook broke out of high schools and universities and went global, Twitter split off on its own independent platform and went global, the most important software you've never heard of, called VM wave, went public. VM wave is what enabled any operating system to work on any computer; it's the foundation of cloud computing. The second most important software you've never heard of called Hadoop was launched. It enables 1 million computers to work together, I think that's called big data. Hadoop didn't invent those algorithms; they were invented by Google, called EFS and MAP reduce. Everyone in business is running these in the background. The third most important software you've never heard of is called Get Up; it's the largest repository of open-source software, with 15 million users and was subsequently bought by Microsoft. Google launched a little-known TV company called YouTube, Google launched its own operating system called Android, IBM launched the world's first cognitive computer called Watson, Jeff Bezos launched the world's first eBook reader (he called it the Kindle). Netflix beamed its first video, the internet crossed 1 billion users, an anonymous Japanese cryptocurrency expert launched a crypto currency called Bitcoin, three design students launched Airbnb, the cost of sequencing the human genome was $100 million in 2001 but falls to $10 million in 2006 and goes off a cliff in 2007 to $100k (and in 2019 is $599). Solar energy took off, as did fracking. The cost of generating a

What the hell happened in 2007!

FRIEDMAN

megabyte of data collapses from $8 to $2.5. Intel for the first time introduced non-silicon materials in its chips.

I believe 2007 will be remembered as one of the single most technological inflection points since Gutenberg."

But the foregoing is far from being value neutral, with much being weighted towards manipulation and control for profit. When convenient, please watch, www.youtube.com/watch?v=LmlbhD6LbSA&t=2123s, from which the following by Daniel Schmachtenberger is drawn:

"In a Society; is health inversely proportionate to how much addiction there is in this Society? And it's interesting that I'm giving an inverse proportionality because it's easier to measure unhealth because health is a lot of complex things, and as we mentioned there are things that drive GDP that are really bad for society like things that drive pollution and war and addiction. And the same is true on the social network. If I make an algorithm that is optimising for anything, I've got to be really, really careful what is being harmed in a theory of trade-offs to optimise for that *thing*... Addiction is always related to some kind of hypernormal stimuli where you get some kind of reward loop... The thing about the hypernormal stimuli is that they increase some type of reward... pleasure in the moment, but actually decrease your sensitivity to lots of other things you might have had happiness towards, i.e., when you're coming down from the heroin you don't really care about friends and sunsets and whatever...

So, you can compel someone's addiction, and you can profit by supplying that narrow *thing* where they are becoming increasingly sensitised to needing that narrow *thing,* desensitised to everything else... So, if you monetise attention, it will fundamentally be bad for people... less sovereignty, less free will, and less choice over their behaviour... The tech is power, and if what is ultimately guiding it is a financial model, and the financial model has the people who are using it as the product to sell information about and to advertisers, and has their attention and behaviour as the product, it can't not be evil."

The business and work ethic, which creates a power boundary between owners and workers (a master-servant relationship) and is sometimes referred to as 'the Protestant work ethic', thereby aligning work with religion, implying that it is good for the soul(!), is founded upon and rooted in capitalist economics, ever-increasing mass consumption resulting from the industrial and technological/information revolutions of the 20th and early 21st centuries, compounded by the more recent multi-media, social-media and information-technology revolutions enacted through a global economy fixated on growth. These are the dominant forces affecting all aspects of our lives, and they can be seen in politics, health, education, charities and businesses alike, and yet such developments are far from being all positive; indeed, many are pathogenic.

Wealth creation (money) coupled with unfettered growth seem to have become the ultimate and sole purpose or mission – ends in themselves – and increasingly the key performance monitors and outcomes are viewed in a purely financial manner, directly attributable to the predatory competitive actions of the *minimal self* indoctrinated by the "propaganda of consumerism", and (see Bernays above) amplified by game theory and reinforced through social media with there being little or no reference to the broader social or ecological environment. Winning is the name of the game: beating your competitors, rivals or colleagues, or achieving what you set out to do, whatever the non-monetary cost or consequences.

Schumacher provides an interesting perspective on economics, and therefore business, when he says: "Economics, which Lord Keynes had hoped would settle down as a modest occupation, similar to dentistry, suddenly becomes the most important subject of all. Economic policies absorb almost the entire attention of government, and at the same time become ever more impotent [as perhaps is reflected in the UK government's BREXIT negotiations and subsequent implementation]. The simplest things cannot get done any more. The richer a society, the more impossible it becomes to do worthwhile things without an immediate pay-off... It tends to absorb the whole of ethics and to take precedence over all other human considerations. Now, quite clearly, this is a pathological development."

Society, as a result, is becoming increasingly dominated by the minimal self; fragmented, selfish, greedy, driven by an egocentric mindset[18] and lacking in any meaningful direction, where practically everything is driven from a business transaction, return on capital or budgetary perspective.

David Edwards, in Free to Be Human, sums up the problems of the last few centuries and the challenges we are currently facing when he says, "Corporate capitalism is fundamentally at odds with life". It is not only at odds with life - it is killing life, in all its forms, especially in humans through increasing poverty. Half the world's population lives on less than $5.50 per day,[19] there is an increasing wealth disparity in which the top10% owns 76% of all wealth whilst the bottom 50% owns just 2%,[20] and ecological degradation is at an all-time high, putting all life on Earth at risk.[21]

Yet some would argue that corporate capitalism and globalisation merely reflect market forces, which are driven by needs and wants of consumers (which, of course, include the 1% and those owning, controlling and managing the System), and therefore, if consumers did not want the negative aspects of the products they buy, then they would simply not buy them – unless, as Bernays says, "We are dominated by the relatively small number of persons that understand the mental processes of the masses. It is they that pull the

…the general population seem somehow to have wandered blindly and apathetically into a state of inertia on such matters, happy to leave the status quo to prevail.

wires [write the algorithms] which control the public mind." A counter to such an argument would contend that:

- If we don't want the consequences of children mining cobalt (used in all mobile devices), getting paid $3.50 a day and facing incredible health hazards, you should not buy mobile devices unless you're happy for such consequences to result. If there really were such a thing as an ethical business, surely such businesses would communicate openly and transparently, advising consumers of the exploitation and harm being done to child workers and the environment, so that they could make informed buying decisions, wouldn't they?

- If we don't want to see fish, sea mammals and sea birds full of plastic, then no one should use plastic bags or plastic bottles, and the advertisements of such products should carry images of the polluted insides of such animals in order that people seen using them would be ostracised, shouldn't they?

- "Facebook knows Instagram is toxic for teen girls [unlikely to be just girls], company documents show. Its own in-depth research shows a significant teen mental health issue that Facebook plays down in public" (WSJ.com, 14 Sept 2021). So, it should be boycotted by users and advertisers, shouldn't it?

- If we can't see past the propaganda, deceit, lies and illusions of these sorcerers (those who exert power and control over us: politicians, global corporations, see p.10 and p.26), we need to pay closer attention, attend to their practice: to what lies behind and to what their ultimate goal is. To hold them to account.

But the general population seem somehow to have wandered blindly and apathetically into a state of inertia on such matters, happy to leave the status quo to prevail.

We need to differentiate here between what we mean by "economics" and "predatory corporate capitalism". Economics is a social science (a social construct created by humankind as opposed to a naturally occurring system or phenomenon) concerned with the production, distribution and consumption of goods and services. Predatory corporate capitalism is an economic system based on private ownership and the rights of private owners. It is dominated by predatory, hierarchical, and bureaucratic corporations that control the factors of production (land, labour, materials, and money) and the amount of profits and capital wealth they generate, the latter being the root cause of extreme inequality and ecological degradation built upon the myth of "maximising shareholder value". Predatory corporate capitalism seeks to subordinate and enslave all other factors (ecological, social, political, media etc.) to its force and its will.

The former is a human construct, an enabling system with no preconditions or predetermined outcomes, whilst the latter utilises the former for its own ends to maximise profits; it is predatory and greedy. The former can also be used for more social, philanthropic and ecological ends, and it is this to which NOW is turning its attention.

The old order of the free market economy, where money is king, where the fittest (richest) will survive and prosper is patently not working – we are destroying our home, planet Earth, and many of her inhabitants. The emergence of extremist politicians, "democratically" elected to lead some of the world's leading economies (though heavily influenced via corporate lobbying, totalitarian governments; China, Russia and others interfering through social media hacking and privately-owned social/news-media corporation moguls), feels as if it might be one final hurrah to keep the old order in place. We can oppose this to a world which lives within its means, sustainably produces its own food, minimises its carbon footprint, and which trades through and within the C.I.C. concept, thereby demonstrating their commitment to a fairer sustainable society rather than just the accumulation of money. Therefore, "affluence" becomes how much someone does for other people and our environment, and the value from taking a philanthropic perspective – rather than how much they can earn for themselves. If money becomes the means to an end (and builds philanthropic C.I.C.s and values philanthropy in general, ultimately replacing money being king) rather than the end in itself, then humankind's base instinct to strive for more can still be fulfilled – but rising to the top of the tree becomes about helping others and our home, planet Earth, rather than just earning money and amassing status symbols for oneself. Therefore, it is a perfectly achievable reality – just a huge change of focus on what is important.

As Lynn Stout of Cornell Law School points out in her article, "The Shareholder Value Myth", "the maxim or idea of corporate capitalism is so deeply ingrained that many people assume corporations are legally required to maximise shareholder value, but this erroneous assumption is thoroughly dispelled." It is here that NOW seeks to make a difference, only having equity providers who support the NOW vision, whilst at the same time getting a limited return from their investment (through forming C.I.C.s under schedule 3 of the Companies Act 2005), utilising affordable debt to fund operations, creating entrepreneurial equity ownership for all involved, and utilising the profit gained to fund philanthropic goals and create more NOW enterprises through C.I.C.s.

When studying the strategic management module for my MBA, two questions were asked in order to help clarify strategic direction: what is our business, and what should our business be? These were obviously asked with specific businesses in mind; however I think both questions are very pertinent for business as a whole. The first question could be answered by saying that, currently, business generally applies pretty much unfettered to: exploitation of labour, thorough inequality, covertly influencing customer behaviour and paying little or no attention to the detrimental ecological impact on our home, planet Earth, in favour of creating assets and monetary wealth for a chosen few. In looking to answer the second question, I turn to Lord Griffiths, who quotes from Pope Benedict's encyclical, which suggests six major ways to make global capitalism more humane.

First, it calls for "The management of globalisation and a reform of international economic institutions." They are needed "To manage the global economy, to revive economies hit by the crisis, to avoid any deterioration of the present [ecological, COVID and post COVID economic recovery, Ukrainian wars economic and social impact] crisis... to guarantee the protection of the environment and to regulate the migration of people not content in their own skin, culture or homeland and are therefore searching." They are searching, generally for the answer in our Western, consumerist, capitalist lifestyle. Not surprisingly, for this huge task we need "A true world political authority", through reform of the United Nations.

"Next, there needs to be greater diversity among the enterprises [e.g., C.I.C.s] that create wealth: mutual societies, credit unions and hybrid forms of commercial organisation. Third, globalisation has weakened the ability of trade unions to represent the interests of workers, something that needs to be reversed. Fourth, the scandal of inequality requires countries to increase the proportion of GDP given as foreign aid.

Fifth, because the environment is the gift of the Creator, we have an intergenerational responsibility to tackle climate change.

Finally, everyone involved in the market – traders, producers, bankers... even consumers – must be alert to the moral consequences of their actions. Development is impossible without upright men and women, without financiers and politicians whose consciences are finely attuned to the common good".

For Pope Benedict, market capitalism can never be conceived of in purely technical terms. "Development is not just about freeing up markets, removing tariffs, increasing investment, and reforming institutions. It is not even about social policies to accompany economic reforms. At the heart of the market is the human person, possessing dignity, deserving of justice, and bearing the divine image. The market needs to be infused with a morality emanating from Christian humanism, which respects truth and encourages charity."

Nearly everything in Pope Benedict's encyclical calls us to act in the image and likeness of God (perfect oneness), holy, whole not as the separate *minimal self* but as a collective united consciousness acting in the best interest of every living creature and our home planet Earth. I am struck by the irony that the word economics literally means 'the art of keeping a house'.

Our current model, as represented by Globalisation, mainly exhibits the major vices:
- Vice: lust, self-indulgence
- Vice: gluttony, over-consumption
- Vice: greed
- Vice: sloth, apathy, carelessness
- Vice: wrath, anger
- Vice: envy
- Vice: pride, ego, selfishness

These need to be replaced with virtues:
- Virtue: self-restraint, knowledge, honesty, wisdom
- Virtue: temperance, self-control, justice, honour
- Virtue: charity; will, generosity, sacrifice
- Virtue: diligence; persistence, effort
- Virtue: patience; peace, mercy, do no harm
- Virtue: kindness; loyalty, compassion, integrity
- Virtue: humility; bravery, modesty, reverence, altruism

The foregoing draws one to consider the perennial question "how should one live one's life", a question which the NOW Movement and Academy facilitates through provocation, challenge and stimulation, seeking possible answers and helping implement solutions. What follows are initial insights as to where such answers and solutions may be sought.

Evolutionary beings

We live in extraordinary times.

This could be said by most generations, as it is obviously grounded in and determined by its context. The paradox of our current time is perhaps that we have never had it so good, measured by global gross domestic product (GDP), and from the proportion of people of an enlightened persuasion, so bad. Both our problems and solutions are encapsulated in the following quote from Jung:

> "In the history of the collective as in the history of the individual, everything depends on the evolution of consciousness."

"Everything depends on the evolution of consciousness" - everything - and it is our primary responsibility to evolve consciousness (both self and collective), through a deeper understanding of perfect oneness, and through the process of enlightenment, for the wellbeing and healing of all.

The beginning of the NOW process (along with the thinking, feeling and motivation that originally inspired it) can be summed up in one word: enlightenment. The etymology of enlightenment is to "remove dimness or blindness" (a primary objective of NOW Academy), and the definition I use here is the process of doing such or moving towards the light.

There is much dimness, darkness, or blindness in the world today, even although we perhaps delude ourselves in believing otherwise. Having already been through the period we called "The Enlightenment" (dominated by the believing in the scientific method and reason) we have perhaps convinced ourselves that we are enlightened and therefore no longer need to pursue enlightenment. Now that we assume we are enlightened, we just get on with it and perpetuate the status quo. Such an attitude towards enlightenment, coupled with the evolutions that resulted from it, has produced a global culture founded upon mass insatiable consumerist growth, the moral laziness of capitalism, and selfish, egocentric mindsets.

A suggested thought to be explored, debated, discussed, and dialogued is whether the Age of Enlightenment was a myth, and whether the subsequent Industrial Revolution has led us to a dead end.

In the majority of religious and spiritual traditions, God is perceived as light. In the Christian Bible, John 8, (12, 14) Jesus says, "I am the light of the world", "I know whence I came, and I know whither I go."

Gabor Mate observes that "If you look at the story about Jesus and Buddha, both of them were tempted by the devil and one of the things that the devil offers them is power, and they both say no because they have the power inside of themselves, they don't need it from the outside. They don't want to control people, they want to teach people by example, not through force. So, they refuse power. Jesus says that the kingdom of God is within, that the power is not outside of yourself but inside. And the Buddha says, "don't worship me, find the land inside yourself, be a lamp unto yourselves, find a light within." What we see and hear at this conference with people sharing information and people receiving information, people committed to a better world, that's actually human nature and what I'm saying to you is that if you find the light within, if you find your own nature then we we'll also be kinder to nature."

So, it would appear to be a plausible strategy to engage in a process that leads from darkness towards the light – enlightenment – and each of us needs to know who we are, from whence we came and whither we go in order to do such.

The state and process of enlightenment is one of deep understanding of what it means to be human, and of our place in the world and the cosmos beyond, but I would suggest our general understanding today is only partial, and is clouded and dominated by the egocentric, modernist, socio-scientific, socio-economic, separated mindset and paradigm deemed suitable for a time gone by, and one that is wholly inappropriate for the 21st century. It is a mindset and paradigm which enslaves us in the trap of believing we either already know, or are governed by those who know, and that we can only simply go on in this paradigm that is created out of an error of the mind which sees "things" as separate, when without a doubt, as much modern day science is proving (for those who need proof), every "thing" is in fact whole, connected, intertwined, fuzzy and unbounded, and it is the egocentric mindset that separates, fragments, imposes and maintains boundaries.

A QUOTE FROM THE CHRISTIAN BIBLE,
CORINTHIANS 13:12, ILLUSTRATES THUS:

For now, we see in
a mirror, darkly; but
then face to face: now
I know in part; but
then I shall know
fully even as also
I was fully known.

AND FROM THE QURAN [10:57]:

The enlightenment
has come to you
herein from your
Lord, and healing for
anything that troubles
your hearts.

In many ways, the world is collapsing environmentally, socially, politically, biologically (i.e., the recent COVID 19 pandemic and the war in Ukraine) and economically - almost a perfect storm of collapsing, as humans simply go on, caught in an ever-increasing egocentric cycle of unsustainable consumption of vital resources, producing mountains of waste. In our broken system, everything finally ends up polluting in landfill, the air or the sea, driven by an insatiable commitment to economic growth calculated by some dubious measure, GDP, with no reference or measurement being applied to wellbeing or ecology, which results in more troubling states of enslavement and ill-being for an ever-larger number of living creatures on our planet.

A quote from Edmund Burke illustrates a key theme which should be a guiding light for the courage and inspiration needed to overcome the apathy and blindness of our times, and also act as an inspiration to us in the NOW family: "The only thing necessary for the triumph of evil is for good men to do nothing."

It is indeed evil to destroy our only means of survival, namely our home, planet Earth, to enslave people through the allure of endless consumption, to subsume all to the power of predatory capitalism and enslave, impoverish and subdue the vast majority of the population as a result. As good men and women we must act and learn to correct this situation.

The only way out of the challenges identified above, or indeed any problem, is through education and learning - through life-long education and learning, through the growth of humanity (all humanity), through learning to be different, and through sustainable development, as the opposite of sustainable development leads to stagnation or decline. Sustainable development could be seen as somewhat of a contradiction in terms, so here we use the phrase 'sustainable future'. To act unsustainably (killing off our future livelihood) has to be insane, and not to act philanthropically (to do harm or act inhumanely) is immoral. Everything is connected; unfettered predatory competition/capitalism breaks this connection and imposes boundaries and establishes winners and losers. The truth is, in fact, this: if one of us loses, we all lose.

A quote from Donald Winnicott illuminates:

> "It is creative apperception more than anything else that makes the individual feel that life is worth living. Contrasted with this is a relationship to external reality which is one of compliance, the world, and its details of being recognised but only as something to be fitted in with our demanding adaptation. Compliance carries with it a sense of futility for the individual and is associated with the idea that nothing matters, and that life is not worth living. In a tantalising way many individuals have experienced just enough

of creative living to recognise that for most of their time they are living uncreatively, as if caught up in the creativity of someone else, or of a machine. This second way of living in the world is recognised as an illness in psychiatric terms. In some way or other our theory includes that living creatively is a healthy state, and that compliance is a sick basis for life."

The majority of our education, learning and development systems and approaches to learning (both children and adult) have been dumbed down and remain fully entrenched in the outmoded purpose, values, principles, techniques, and practices associated with a pathogenic, socio-economic, socio-scientific paradigm predicated upon dominance, power, and control. A recent quote from the World Economic Forum illuminates this by pointing out that "Our education system is broken. The way we educate future generations no longer prepares them adequately for the skills and jobs of today [so why do we perpetuate it?]. The idea that you study maths and science and art in your youth as separate disciplines, and then work to solve real world problems in today's economy, does not add up. Preparing students for tomorrow's jobs requires breaking down the silos within education." Such systems and processes are not fit for current purposes, and they are based solely on anthropocentricism. If one wants to perpetuate the status quo, one needs to be elsewhere, as here we are creating the future and living up to what it means to be human... but what does it mean to be human?

A call for change: continuous sustainable evolution starting with a [r]evolution in self-consciousness and collective consciousness (mindset and culture), which we need to address through the approach articulated herein, and which is well illuminated in the following video by Giles Hutchins: www.youtube.com/watch?v=t2mUebq5PXU&feature=youtu.be

Please DO NOT read further until you have viewed it. The quote towards the end of this video, from John Naisbitt, when he says "The greatest breakthroughs of the 21st century will not happen through technology but through an ever-expanding concept of what it means to be human" (i.e. the expansion of what it means to be human through an ever deepening awareness, experience, observation, action and personal practice) is particularly relevant to us. It is what the NOW Academy is all about; not in some anthropocentric or purely intellectual way, but in a holistic, harmonious, grounded and inclusive way.

It is only through [r]evolution in consciousness toward enlightenment embraced from within in a NOW paradigm grounded in the definition of Action Research (see p.156) that we stand the best chance of enacting what it means to be human – along with any chance of surviving and sustaining

**99.9 percent of everything
you think and of everything
you do is for yourself
and there isn't one.**

WEI WU WEI

our existence. Once self-consciousness changes, everything changes. Just imagine what would happen if the self-consciousness of leaders of the world's businesses and political parties changed to embrace NOW principles!

So, what does it mean to be human, to live a virtuous human life?

This is obviously an open, evolutionary, and emergent question as humans continue to evolve through a process of becoming and learning, moving towards truth through deep knowledge, learning and wisdom. It is also clearly an anthropological question, as it is humans asking the question to which answers can only be formulated from reflections, interpretations and selected narratives of the past. Humans are an important element of nature, and we need to connect and resonate with everything. We need to cohere. We need to remember where we have come from and our connection with everything. We are in part stardust, earth, plant, animal and soul, and they are – in part – us. We are interlinked and integrated through a process of relating with everything we come in to contact with.

Here are some perspectives on living a virtuous human life:

Life is relating; it is organic. It is relating with parents and ancestors, the bacteria that comprise us, friends, teachers, mentors, role models, the food that we eat, the air that we breathe, the water we drink, the knowledge we attain; indeed, everything and everyone we come into contact with defines, refines, shapes, and reshapes what we label as 'I', 'we', 'us', and 'that'.

Life is a knitting-together, the weaving of a tapestry, an emergent building-on what has gone before, an education, an evolution.

Life is journey. We enter the world with gifts to give, and to realise our own unique purpose. The journey of life is to realise our gifts and to live our purpose. The journey is a process of becoming.

Life is choice. As we realise our emerging and evolving web of relating, we must have the freedom to choose which relationships resonate with our purpose and our gifts, and so embrace and cultivate them so that we may become who we are born to be, and to discard those that are dissonant and which we must let go of in order to remain healthy.

A life well lived, therefore, is a life that forges positive relating, makes the choices that ensure our collective wellbeing and unfolds our gifts, thereby enabling our purpose.

Life is self-realisation - the realisation that there is no self.

Cleary, to understand the human condition we must gain a perspective on the human psyche, as it is fundamental to self (relatedness)-awareness, and for this we turn to the Swiss psychiatrist Carl Jung.

Jung's definition of psyche: "By psyche I understand the totality of all psychic processes, conscious as well as unconscious, (CW6 para 797) so I use the term 'psyche' rather than 'mind', since mind is used in common parlance to refer to the aspects of mental functioning which are conscious." Jung maintained that the psyche is a self-regulating system (like the body).

Jung postulates that the psyche strives to maintain a balance between opposing qualities while at the same time actively seeking its own development, or as he called it, "Individuation", which is the search for wholeness within the human psyche. It may be described as a process of circumambulation around the Self as the centre of personality. The person aims to become conscious of him or herself as a unique human being, but at the same time, no more nor less than any other human being.

Individuation describes how Jung's teleological agency concept of self works. Jung saw it as the process of self-realisation, the discovery and experience of meaning and purpose in life; the means by which one finds oneself and becomes who one really is. It depends upon the interplay and synthesis of opposites, e.g. conscious and unconscious, personal and collective, psyche and soma, divine and human, life and death. Individuation is dependent upon relating. The self is relational.

> "The self is relatedness... The self only exists inasmuch as you appear. Not that you are, but that you do the self. The self appears in your deeds and deeds always mean relationship."[22]

In Jeff Lieberman's talk, he says "I am moving at the speed of light, and I am the age of the universe."

Steiner: "The human being is not an idle onlooker before the pageant of the world, mirroring back in his spirit what is going on in the universe without involving him; he is an active participant in a cosmic creative process and his knowledge is actually the most highly evolved part of the organism of the universe."

St Francis of Assisi: "What you are looking for is what is looking."

Lee Smolin: "The situation of human life is to be balanced between danger and opportunity and when the future is unknown how do we think usefully about the future and I think if we imagine ourselves living in a cosmos where novelty is an illusion, agency is an illusion, will is an illusion that there's a demoralisation and alienation that takes place between our aspirations and our view of the universe we live in.

The self is relatedness...
The self only exists
inasmuch as you appear.
Not that you are, but that
you do the self. The self
appears in your deeds
and deeds always mean
relationship.

JUNG

If we imagine ourselves living in a universe in which everything changes and everything evolves in which novelty is a real possibility in which the imagination that takes advantage of the natural capacity to invent novel phenomena and for novel regularities to arise then we may get a moral life we may even if we can see how it is possible that we may have the agency, the imagination, the will to invent a solution out of the problems that face us."

St Augustine. "Our whole business in this life is to restore to health the eye of the heart whereby God may be seen." Whereby we may become enlightened.

The following are a selection of answers to the question "what is life" proposed by contributors on www.humansandnature.org

STEPHAN HARDING

"The experiences of meditators and contemplatives over the centuries and, more recently, of Western psychologists such as Jung and Hillman have shown us that we operate from two fundamental (and interrelated) levels or modes of consciousness: what we might call a limited, shallow, self-centred level of consciousness, and an expansive, deep/wide, ecocentric level of consciousness.

The first is the everyday mind of our common experience in which it seems to us that we are nothing more than isolated, solidly existing "selves" that we must protect at all costs from a hostile world. In this mode, our main priority is the safeguarding of own comfort and wellbeing, often attained to the detriment of those around us and of the living world that enfolds us, to which we are mostly indifferent.

This self-centred state is absolutely natural, and without it we would perish, but it becomes dangerous when we are told, as we are in Western civilization, that this is all there is to being human: that even our most altruistic acts can be explained by a reduction to our "selfish" genes and their urge to propel themselves as "units of selection" into future generations. Our entire modern civilization is built on the cultivation of self-centeredness. We see it everywhere: in the cult of celebrity, in the idea that we can only discover who we truly are by buying the right industrial products at ever-accelerating rates and by accumulating more and more material wealth with which to buy them.

When Deng Xiaoping said to his nation that "To be rich is glorious", he initiated a massive avalanche of selfishness and greed in China that is sweeping the entire planet closer to ecological catastrophe.

We have made highly dangerous choices in using our well-honed capacities for scientific, analytical reasoning in service of our self-centred mode of consciousness. We have chosen to use science to create immensely powerful technologies that have given us the freedom to extract and manipulate wild molecules from the body of the Earth in ways that are creating severe problems for all living beings, including the planet herself.

We seem set on continuing to make these choices despite overwhelming scientific evidence about their detrimental effects. Mere information is not enough to break through our self-centred consciousness, which only intensifies as the economic growth model tightens its grip, strangling our collective imagination. The result is the severe alienation of the human psyche from nature that is increasingly symptomatic of our times.

Experiencing our full humanity requires us to attenuate our self-centeredness by enfolding it within a much wider sense of self in which we experience genuine love and compassion for all beings, both living and non-living. There are many names for this wider, deeper self, which is our deepest level of consciousness. My preference is for Arne Naess's term ecological self because it suggests that the wider self is not some insubstantial, ethereal intellectualization, but rather deeply rooted in the very materiality of our planet, in its teeming biodiversity, its ancient, crumpled continents, its swirling atmosphere, and the depths and shallows of its lakes, rivers, and oceans. Thus, the ecological self is not only the human self. It is also the self or soul of the world, the anima mundi that awakens us to our full humanity; when we know, palpably, in our very bones, that there is a selfhood far more vast than the one in which we live and have our being, and to which we are ultimately accountable. Jung succinctly gives us a taste of this when he says, "At times I feel as if I am spread over the landscape and inside things, and am myself living in every tree, in the splashing of the waves, in the clouds and the animals that come and go, in the procession of the seasons."

When we are thus "spread over the landscape", we feel that nature is animate – that it is imbued with intelligence, wisdom, and a communicative ability that make us feel a natural inclination to minimize harm to the greater self that enfolds and nurtures us. From this level of consciousness, we make choices that minimize harm to the greater body of the Earth, which we experience as our own body. We opt for simplicity and frugality in our material consumption and cultivate richness and diversity in our cultural and spiritual lives, where we realize that true satisfaction lies.

Thus, the most pressing challenge for our times is to awaken the ecological selves of as many people as possible within the shortest possible time. It is vitally important to help people to fall in love with the Earth, by whatever peaceful means possible. I am not at all optimistic that we will be able to do this, but we must each do what we can in our own limited spheres of life. Theorizing about our ecological predicament is, at best, only a beginning.

A vital practice is to spend time alone, in silence, outdoors in as wild a place as one can find, allowing the sensuous language of nature to dissolve away our civilization's corrosive notion that nature is no more than a mute, inert machine. Perhaps it might then dawn on us that we are fully human only when we deeply love and respect not only other humans, but also the vast other-than-human world that enfolds and sustains us."

THROSTUR EYSTEINSSON

"We tell stories. Some are true, most are not. We are only marginally adept at telling the difference. Science is an attempt at a system to get the story right. It sometimes works. Lies (in a broad sense) are not less interesting and certainly not less useful than true stories. They help us attract mates, maintain social cohesion, and allow us to feel good about ourselves.

From deviousness to entertainment to bull (an old Norse word meaning gibberish and not its homonym meaning male bovine, the confusion of the two having resulted in the term "bullshit," which is actually a stronger term – see, I told a story), telling untrue stories has resulted in development of our imaginations, whether by biological or cultural evolution.

Our developed imaginations give us the ability to anticipate the future, to predict, but not to do much about it, as in the case of climate change. Sometimes, the things we imagine and stories we tell promote positive social development and technological progress, sometimes the outcomes are negative. Many instances of both can be found, for example in our dealings with the rest of nature. Telling stories about things getting better does not mean that they will get better, but it might be a necessary precondition."

ALISA RAMIREZ

"What it means to be human....

To live for someone else, to strive for greatness yet give up everything in an instant for that person. To reproduce and love an innocent creation. It is natural to feel accomplishment in life when you help another person. Life has meaning when you LOVE. Compassion...

Understanding the human mind and body is to feel the connection between the earth/nature and human beings... how the earth and gravitational shifts changes us. The cause and effect, the changes that occur in our minds and bodies, with our emotions due to changes in mother nature... to gain a sense of wellness within oneself, self-evaluation, the ability to be in control of your emotions.

Knowing and understanding that the connection of one human being to another through physical touch is needed to survive when we enter this life as infants. Without that connection, without that touch sending feelings of comfort that another life is there to guide, love, and protect you. Knowing what it is to BE human, and how powerful and amazing our minds and bodies are; how they adapt through environmental changes. WE are amazing beings."

Indigenous (meaning originating or occurring naturally in a particular place) people know what they are and their authentic connection with their environment. They are Arne Ness's "ecological self" and Jung's "experience of being", and they don't need to 'find themselves'. The people of the 'developed' world have an intellect which is alien (meaning remote or separate), and which dominates 21st-century culture represented by globalisation and social media and seem to be ever trying to "find themselves". We need to build an indigenous culture in order to overcome our existential problems and to thrive.

"Sooner or later, nuclear physics and the psychology of
the unconscious will draw closer together, as both of them
independently of one another and from opposite directions,
push forward into transcendental territory."
Jung

ELEMENT TWO

Insights into the
human condition: perfect
oneness, consciousness,
mind, thought, thinking
and awareness.

Introduction

Clearly, it is vitally important for those who are interested, involved or engaged in the NOW Movement from whatever perspective or context to have a reasonably shared understanding of the following interpretations in order to engage and develop.

The initial central tenets upon which NOW stands are those of non-duality: one undivided, without a second, and emergence (from the Latin; bring towards the light).

In looking to describe non-duality, it is perhaps useful to look at what duality (or separateness) is, and Spira describes this well when he says:

"Duality is the belief, and more importantly the feeling, that experience is divided into two essential ingredients, the part that knows it and another part that is known, one part does the experiencing and another part that is experienced. The part that knows is what we call 'I', 'myself', and it is believed or more importantly felt to reside in the body and to be identical with the body and the part that is known or experienced is considered to be everything else, objects, others, and the world. 'I', the inside subject knowing 'you' or 'it' the outside object. This fundamental presumption is so deeply embedded in the way we think and feel very few of us realise that it is in fact a presumption, we take it to be the absolute fact of experience and upon this apparent certainty almost everything we think, feel and do is based. We may question many things in our life, but few people ever question this fundamental presumption. It is considered so obviously true as to require no further investigation. We investigate almost everything else but the fundamental presumption upon which almost all our thoughts and feelings and subsequent activities and relationships are based is seldom questioned." But why do we take this presumption to be ultimately true. Much of what follows seriously questions this notion.

If you are embarrassed
by the word spirit,
think of spirit as the
subtlest form of matter
but if you are embarrassed
by the word matter, think
of it as the densest
form of spirit.

SRI AUROBINDO

Emergence is a process whereby larger entities, patterns and regularities arise through interactions among smaller or simpler entities that themselves do not exhibit such properties i.e., that over 50% of a human being is made up of bacteria, viruses, fungi and archaea but we take the totality of this bacteria to be a human being. It is from within these central, innately creative tenets that NOW is seeking to cause a paradigm shift in our understanding and application of what it means to be human, our place in the world and the cosmos beyond, thereby correcting our past errors and creating a sustainable, thriving future. It is the egocentric mindset that has separated and fragmented what is essentially whole, taken that fragmentation, measured, labelled, defined and refined it, and then utilised the results as a definitive description from which to discern a unitarist reality, one existing outside us and which is totally separate from us. We then use these descriptions and results to manipulate and control, we further compound this error of separation, [23] even as the holy grail of materialist proof, scientific belief, is now postulating otherwise, which further suggests the current generally accepted version of reality is a socio-cultural construct that we, or those "pulling the wires" are choosing to maintain.

> "Only the existence of a field of force can account for the motions of bodies observed, and its assumption dispenses with space curvature. All literature on this subject is futile and destined to oblivion. So are all attempts explain the workings of the universe without recognising the existence of the ether [maybe dark matter, pure consciousness, strings within the ether] and the indispensable function it plays in the phenomena.
>
> My second discovery was of a physical truth of greatest importance. As I have searched the entire scientific records in more than half a dozen languages for a long time without finding the least anticipation, I consider myself the original discoverer of this truth, which can be expressed by the statement: There is no energy in matter other than received from the environment [inter-connectedness, wholeness].
>
> If you want to find the secrets of the universe, think in terms of energy, frequency and vibration and the day science begins to study non-physical phenomena, it will make more progress in one decade than in all previous centuries of its existence."
> *Nikola Tesla*

An idea of theoretical quantum physics is known as string theory, which intuitively sounds to me a useful metaphor to aid our thinking here. It postulates that all matter is made up of energy and that energy is derived from strings which vibrate as waves at different frequencies. As with many scientific theories, the detail surrounding them can be complex and dominated by experts. For a layman's interpretation please now view: www.youtube.com/watch?v=eGxPGgPdTVw and www.youtube.com/watch?v=yoUcrGncBTo.

According to string theory, absolutely everything in the universe – all of the particles that make up all matter and all energy and all forces underlying such, including consciousness – are comprised of tiny vibrating fundamental strings. Moreover, every one of these strings is identical. The only difference between one string and another, whether it's a heavy particle that is part of an atom or a massless particle that carries light, is its resonant pattern, or how it vibrates. The strings or waves either vibrate chaotically, through their vibrating interactions – or through human (or non-human) interaction, through our conscious actions – collapse into matter through observance (measurement[24]). Self-consciousness is one such observer bringing things into being; it is creative.

> "The creative person is one who brings something from the unknown into the world of the known, who brings something from God into the world, who helps God to utter something – who becomes a hollow bamboo and allows God to flow through him. How can you become a hollow bamboo? If you are too full of the mind, you cannot become a hollow bamboo. And creativity is from the creator, creativity is not of you or from you. You disappear, then creativity is – when the creator takes possession of you."
> *Osho*

The strings can manifest as particles (matter) or as waves (energy). The question of what a particle is and what is a wave is an interesting, somewhat magical one. Heisenberg's uncertainty principle shows "that the interaction between the observing apparatus and what is observed [measured] always involves an exchange of one or more invisible [perhaps Tesla's field, Bohm's implicit order or what I call perfect oneness] and uncontrollably fluctuating quanta" (Bohm). These strings vibrate as a superposition of nodes. Quantum superposition states that the quantum system, which underlies all, is in multiple states at the same time, until it is measured. As John Archibald Wheeler's delayed choice experiment shows, a photon's behaviour is not predetermined the act of observance and measurement determines the result, and it is humans doing much of the observing and measuring.

It is interesting to note that the root of the word 'measurement' comes from the Sanskrit word 'Maya' (illusion), so in some sense we are creating illusions which we then treat as our determined reality, which can be both an opportunity and a threat.

Elliot Grant Watson writes: "I have become aware of what Jung has called "the noumenal reality" which embraces the whole situation." which includes the observer and the observed. Stedall goes a step further: "the observer and the observed are in their innermost essence one and the same thing." [perfect oneness, unified field of influence]. Geoffrey Chew comments: "Science no longer holds any absolute truths. Even the discipline of physics whose laws once went unchallenged has had to submit to the indignity of the uncertainty principle. In this climate of disbelief, the old distinction between natural and supernatural has become meaningless." Diarmuid O'Murchu, a Roman Catholic priest, further comments: "But something much deeper is resurfacing in the emerging consciousness of our time, namely, we are our relationships." – we are the vibration.

Natural philosophy (which we now call science), our main method of mapmaking employed to describe what appears, is increasingly looking mind-like (consciousness-like). It creates images, metaphors, pictures, thoughts and visions, and determines them as dualistic absolute deterministic reality. However, quantum mechanics (a finer level of detail to our mapmaking) is pointing to the underlying nature of everything as being fluctuating quanta (wholeness), and this produces a paradox between duality (separateness) and the underlying wholeness, and this paradox is the cause of all humankind's confusions and challenges. Indeed, as we shall see later, some scientists (Hoffman in particular p.85) are hypothesising that consciousness (mind) is fundamental. Hoffman uses a metaphor to describe this mapmaking as like the icons of a computer screen; they are an interface recognisable to human beings but are nothing like the underlying process that enables their depiction. One of the elements contained in our quantum-mechanical metaphor (one of our evolving maps) is that of wave function,[25] which is, from my perspective, a form of fluctuating quanta: the strings. Strings appear to underlie all forms and may indeed be consciousness itself. Should the foregoing be true then all is primordial consciousness (perfect oneness) that is continuing to awaken and evolve, and humankind should aid such and must not fall back into the patterns of the separated, ego-based, material world/culture that we have created and maintained to date, and which has brought about our current existential challenges.

Based on the above, it would appear there is no distinction between subjective and objective, material and energy, inside and outside, or observer and object. Such duality is constructed by humans through our senses, our classifications and our projections.

The way we choose to interact with the universe therefore determines the result. This makes us very powerful and very creative. We choose how and when to collapse some, or maybe, just maybe, all of the wave function into material form, socially-constructed thoughts and culture and we create the boundaries for our own ends, but the key word is choice: we can choose between conflict and peace, separateness and wholeness, inequality and equality, sustainability and unsustainability, evil and good, poverty and abundance, and other things besides.

We then create the stories, beliefs, religions, social systems and culture in support of our choices, and then call them reality; a reality that we believe that is either too hard to change or one we deny that we have the ability to change. Please now view www.youtube.com/watch?v=SF4OxulBDuk presented by Deepak Chopra before reading further.

I once heard Satish Kumar, previously a Jain monk, and latterly an environmentalist, give a lecture at Lancaster University in which he quoted Descartes' "I think therefore I am" before going on to ask who is this "I" and what is all this "thinking". Again, until we have a shared understanding of these "I" and "thinking" concepts, it is very difficult to engage in any meaningful way. Some of what follows provides a reasonable perspective from which to start to gain such an understanding.

In the next two sections I draw on and slightly paraphrase insights provided by the work of Spira in articulating the works of Advanta Vedanta, a Hindu philosophy and religious practice which refers to the idea that the soul (true self, Atman, self-consciousness) is the same as the highest metaphysical reality (Brahman, perfect oneness), which resonates strongly with the quantum phenomenon and non-duality, string and unified field theories expressed in these sections, as we "Push forward into transcendental territory" Jung.

The soul is the reflection of the underlying consciousness/perfect oneness,[26] the "I am". My spirit is the metaphorical voice by which my soul manifests and reflects through my body-mind. The separation and labelling of these elements is obviously dualistic, and I am separating them for illustrative purposes only.

Throughout my research on the subject matter herein I have been struck by the strong resonances of non-duality – 'oneness' – with many religions and philosophies, which also concur with the theme of the following sections.

Finite and Infinite

Something which we call finite we determine as having clear boundaries and as limited in thought, time and space. By contrast, the infinite is unbounded and unlimited, an indivisible infinite reality underlying all.

One of the conundrums for human beings is to grasp the concept of, let us say, an infinite universe. We think surely it must have a limit, but what would that be? If we apply our thinking to this, we can immediately see that our experience of our existence is through our finite mind and our finite senses. All that we experience is finite, such as the fact that light entering our retina is converted into neural signals which produce an image in our brains (see Hoffman above), or the way our eyes determine light as colour, but we don't see the full light spectrum.

All of our awareness, our minds, our thoughts and experiences are finite, partial, and cannot experience or be fully aware of the infinite, and we therefore tend to ignore it, as with "dark matter" and "all other things being equal," and therefore we live in our finite constructions.

Our perceptions of tangible, objective, separate objects are taken to be finite at what we determine to be the gross level, but as we know, at the most subtle level, they are all made up of vibrating energy (the strings of string theory). What we take for an absolute, unitarist external reality is a product of our finite senses and our finite minds; it is a reality we are creating, constructing, or co-creating, but it is not the ultimate reality that is infinite. However, the fact that we cannot fully experience the infinite does not mean it is not there or that it is not having an impact – and perhaps a major impact – on us. In fact, the infinite is the ultimate (perfect oneness), from within which the finite manifests.

We are not so much
in fear of our own
limitations [finite] but
the infinite within us.

UNKNOWN

If the doors of
perception were cleansed,
everything would appear
to man as it is, infinite.
For man has closed
himself up, till he sees all
things through narrow
chinks of his cavern.

WILLIAM BLAKE

An interesting thought experiment drawn from insights from Advanta Vedanta (see video below) is to consider where and when my experience and awareness (self-consciousness) take place. It can only ever be "now" and "here", from within the finite mind, because have you ever experienced anything other than "now" or "here"? A few lines from Wagoner's poem, "Lost", on page 19, illuminates further: "wherever you are is called here, and you must treat it as a powerful stranger, must ask permission to know it and be known". "Here" is indeed powerful, as it is all we have, along with our ability to fully "know it" and "be known", to know who we are and to show our authentic self "here" and "now". Our experience is teeming with information. Just consider all the information from particles, light waves, heat and cold, – among other things – that is bombarding our incredibly complex brains, with their 100 billion neurons and 1000 trillion synapses. Through our interaction with it all, from within the quantum unified field (manifesting as the forest in the poem "Lost"), we determine ourselves and reality. Clearly there is only an ever-present "now" and an ever-present "here", with anything else being a selected memory or a selected and imagined vision.

What is the difference between all these "now's" and "here's"? Are there lots of "now's" and "here's", and if so, how long are they and where are they? Are they all the same length or point in time and space, and if we add them all together when do we get to infinity? And if so, how many "now's" and "here's" do we need to reach infinity? How long does "now" and "here" last?

They cannot possibly be different, because this "now" and this "here" are the only "now" and the only "here" that exist, and there can only be one "now" and one "here". It is our experience and awareness from within our finite mind that differentiates, which projects and remembers. "Now" and "here" have no duration in time or space and are therefore infinite.

Indeed, in some way they are one and the same.

Our finite mind, awareness and experience can only arise out of the infinite (perfect oneness, the unified field), and collapse back into it, just like the sea arising as a wave only to return to the ocean.

Thought cannot really think about "now" or "here" because thought is finite and cannot fully grasp that which is infinite. Thought cannot think of the "now" and "here" because thought can only know a finite object. The "now" and "here" have no objective limited qualities and therefore cannot be thought about. When convenient please watch Spira at https://www.youtube.com/watch?v=df9YPTe14nU from which the foregoing insights were drawn and paraphrased. It is perhaps best experienced as a meditation, so watch it somewhere you won't be disturbed.

"Now" and "here" are always present. "Now" and "here" are not moments in time or places in space; they have nothing to do with time and space and indeed time and space are human constructs. Hoffman is also postulating that consciousness was fundamental even before the Big Bang, and if he is correct, it is consciousness which spreads out, wave-like, through the infinite unified field, or perhaps is itself the unified field. Perhaps it is the infinite unified field from within which we determine "now" and "here" and label it our own experience of being. It is always "now" and "here" when "I am (self)", and "I am" is eternally "now" and eternally "here". The "now" and "here" is "I am" and "I am" is awareness, which we shall label self-consciousness (consciousness expressed through the finite self).

To reiterate and quote Spira, "Time is eternity filtered [and created] through thought, space is infinity filtered [and created] through perception. Time is eternal consciousness objectified by thought, space is eternal, infinite consciousness [perfect oneness] objectified by perception" (made finite). "Here" and "now" (made finite) are experienced in awareness, awareness is always present, "here" and "now" is the experience of being aware, is awareness, is self-consciousness that shines in each of us, as the knowledge "I am" "here" and "now" is where "I am". "Here" and "now" are the self being conscious, aware."

Bohm, one of the most insightful and inspiring authors I have ever read, provides a good insight to the finite and infinite.

> "In considering the relationship between the finite and the
> infinite, we are led to observe that the whole field of the finite is
> inherently limited, in that it has no independent existence. It has
> the appearance of independent existence, but that appearance
> is merely the result of an abstraction of our thought. We can see
> this dependent nature of the finite from the fact that every finite
> thing is transient.
>
> Our ordinary view holds that the field of the finite is all that
> there is. But if the finite has no independent existence, it cannot
> be all that is. We are in this way led to propose that the true
> ground of all being is the infinite, the unlimited; and the infinite
> includes and contains the finite. In this view, the finite, with its
> transient nature, can only be understood as held suspended, as it
> were, beyond time and space, within the infinite.
>
> The field of the finite is all we can see, hear, touch, remember
> and describe. This field is basically that which is manifest or
> tangible. The essential quality of the infinite, by contrast, is its
> subtlety, its intangibility. This quality is conveyed in the word
> *spirit*, whose root meaning is "wind or breath". This suggests an
> invisible but pervasive energy, to which the manifest world of the
> finite responds. This energy, or spirit, infuses all living beings,

and without it any organism must fall apart into its constituent elements. That which is truly alive in the living being is the energy of spirit, and this is never born and never dies."

The final paragraph of this quote resonates well with Goethe, "I praise what is truly alive."

So, the finite which we formulate in mind can only manifest within the infinite because infinite is all encompassing. Emilie du Chatelet proved that energy cannot be created or destroyed, and it must therefore be infinite. What's more, as everything is made from energy, there can be no such thing as nothing (no-thing, see comments from Dirac below); energy is just constantly changing form, therefore nothing dies - it just changes form. "Nothing can come out of nothing; and nothing that exists can become nothing" Parmenides. "All is constant flow (Panta rhei)" Heraclitus. It is our separate mind that creates something and nothing; all dualities: life-death, beginning-end, subjective-objective, etc.

Here is an interesting take on nothing, the vacuum or void, from Jim Al-Khalili.[27]

"Empty space? No such thing as nothing. Paul Dirac theorised the anti-electron: the mirror image of an electron (which has opposite properties), and an electron, and an anti-electron could form part of an anti-atom and many anti-atoms could fit together to make an anti-matter table or even an anti-matter me [an anti-matter anything]. Dirac realised if things and anti-things ever met each other, they would instantly annihilate each other, turning all their mass into energy and would disappear completely.

Heisenberg suggested that matter could pop into existence for incredibly short periods of time, and then Dirac provided the mechanism by which matter could be created out of the vacuum, and just as quickly disappear again. Whenever a particle pops out of empty space, so (simultaneously) does its anti-particle. Although this sounds completely ridiculous, let me assure you that it is true. Empty space is always awash with these fluctuations. Within nothingness, there is a kind of fizziness – a kind of dance – as pairs of particles and anti-particles borrow energy from the vacuum for brief moments before annihilating and paying it back again. The vacuum goes from a place of being nothing to being a place teeming with matter and anti-matter creations. Dirac's ideas about empty space were refined and developed into what is known today as quantum field theory. So, it seems nothingness is in fact a seething mass of virtual particles appearing and disappearing trillions of times in the blink of an eye.

Everywhere in the universe, space is filled with a vacuum that has this deep mysterious energy. When using the mathematics laid out by Heisenberg

No such thing as nothing

AL-KHALILI

and running the real, physical experiments, the answer you get matches the theory to one part in a million. The theory of quantum mechanics is the most accurate and powerful description of the natural world that we have.

As the universe sprang from the vacuum it expanded very rapidly, and this means that the rules of the quantum world should have contributed to the large-scale structure of the entire cosmos. When our universe first came into existence it was many times smaller than a single atom, and down at this size it is governed not by the classical rules we are familiar with, but by the weird rules of the quantum world. It's quantum reality that has shaped the structure of the universe we see today. Our universe is just the quantum world inflated many, many times. Nothing really has shaped everything.

The WMAP space mission team produced a picture (see video mentioned in bibliography) of the first light that was released after the Big Bang. Think of it as a baby photo of everything; like taking a picture of an embryo at twelve hours after conception compared to taking a picture of a person who is fifty years old. It is the same perspective.

The scars left by the quantum vacuum on our universe – these irregularities created in the first moments of existence by the teeming quantum vacuum – meant that the matter of the universe didn't spread out completely evenly. Rather, it formed vast clumps that would evolve into the galaxies and clusters of galaxies that make up the universe today.

The application of quantum physics to cosmology was revolutionary. It really changed our entire perception of the universe. It provides a natural mechanism through quantum fluctuations to see the early universe with small irregularities that later grow to make galaxies. The thought is really overwhelming that an object with billions of stars like the milky way began life as a quantum fluctuation. An object of such microscopic scale is mind boggling.

It now appears as if the quantum world has actually shaped everything. Something that was a tiny fluctuation [similar to miniscule trace, see p.23] becomes our galaxy, in a cluster of galaxies. These fluctuations are the seeds that grew into the universe we see today; the seeds that made every human being. At the beginning of time, the universe sprang from the vacuum, creating not only vast amounts of matter but also the strange stuff that was predicted by Dirac: anti-matter.

But the universe we see today is made of matter. Nearly all of the anti-matter seems to have vanished. The Big Bang produced equal amounts of matter and anti-matter but as the universe cooled down, matter and anti-matter almost annihilated perfectly (but not quite). For every billion particles of matter and anti-matter, one was left behind, and it was these that made stars and galaxies and people. So, we are simply the debris of the huge annihilation of matter and anti-matter at the beginning of time, the leftovers of an unimaginable explosion.

What we once thought of as the void [vacuum] now seems to hold within it the deepest mysteries of the entire universe. There is a profound connection between the nothingness from which we originated and the infinite within which we are engulfed."

Perfect oneness

Perfect oneness is infinite, without dimensions, limits or forms; it is the fundamental essence underlying all objects, subjects, thoughts, knowledge, awareness's and experiences; it encompasses everything and all.

Self-consciousness (finite, awareness, experience, mind and thought) arises within and through perfect oneness as the finite mind in each of us, and is reflected, created and adopted by human minds in finite time and finite space. Everything at its source is perfect oneness, which is currently reflected and labelled at the subtlest level by the finite mind through the application of scientific beliefs as the strings of string theory or the unified field. To some (reflected by the finite mind; self-consciousness), perfect oneness may well appear to be the harmony of the strings, arising as a background noise, a distant memory; perfect oneness playing itself when in fact it is they, us, perhaps, who are the harmony being played. The strings or unified field are different dualistic labels humans have attributed to describe the underlying infinite perfect oneness.

Perfect oneness has been seen by many, including the French philosopher Henri Bergson, the psychologist William James, and the Swiss philosopher Jean Gerber "Not as a result of neurons and molecules, but as responsible for them", in the words of Stedall.

For the rest of this book, I would like to use the meaning that Bohm ascribes to "Spirit" (or soul) - "an invisible but pervasive energy to which the manifest world of the future responds". It started with the Big Bang, and ever-emerging and evolving, it is implicit and innate, all and everything - to depict perfect oneness as it manifests itself in our finite constructed realities and influenced to a greater or lesser degree by self-consciousness through our choosing. Time and space are constructs of the finite mind and have nothing to do with what perfect oneness is. Perfect oneness is the ground of our essential being, the ground of all.

An invisible but pervasive energy, to which the manifest world of the finite responds.

BOHM

"What is consistently present in the "now" and "here"? Awareness is always present in the "now" and "here" which shines in each of us as I am" Spira (see p.84). In the earliest pages of the Torah, influencing both Judaism and Christianity, God tells Moses "This is the name I shall be known as for all future generations; I am that I am". The "I am" by which God is to be known, in the context of this book is perfect oneness, infinite omnipresence (Spirit) and also non-dualistic. It spreads out wave-like, especially if you place a comma after the "that", which would imply that God is in everything, and that everything is made in the image and likeness of God. Namaste: I praise the Perfect Oneness within you, within me, within all.

It may well be that humans can directly experience spirit or indeed return to the mind of God, the ground of our essential being; but in doing so, we would return to perfect oneness and the self would no longer exist. This is perhaps what happens when we die: we return to the mind of God, we return home (see Amoda Maa Jeevan p.162). There are examples of such throughout religious history, including miracles, ascensions and manifestations.

Eckhart Tolle provides further insight into our understanding of perfect oneness through what he calls "Perfect consciousness". "One consciousness. Unconditional loving presence. It's not the physical form we love but what inhabits the physical form, which is the essence, the organising principal, the intelligence that keeps all the molecules and atoms together. Science, at the moment, equates life with matter but life is beyond matter and ultimately life is consciousness [perfect oneness], an expression of the one [non-dual, God] consciousness.

A single consciousness [infinity] is totally incomprehensible to the human mind.

Many of the world's religions emphasise a suffering God; Jesus suffered. The image of a suffering God is deeply significant because this suffering is everybody. Suffering is what every life form goes through when it assumes the seemingly separate material form. Some ancient teachings say that consciousness fell into matter, into form, seemingly different forms".

All life, therefore, is an expression of the one consciousness [perfect oneness, the Christ in you]. All matter and energy [which are interchangeable $E=MC2$] is the one consciousness expressing itself. The one consciousness, just like energy and information, cannot be destroyed or die; it just changes form. This is very well expressed in a novel by John Green and a series broadcast on BBC iPlayer, *Looking for Alaska*, on the death of Alaska:

"If you take her genetic code and you add her life's experiences and the relationships she had with people and then you take the size and shape of her body you do not get her. There is something else entirely. There's a part of her greater than the sum of her knowable parts and that part has to go somewhere because energy [matter, information] once created is never destroyed. We cannot be born, and we cannot die. We can only change shapes and sizes and manifestations. To be continued..." Such sentiments support Tolle's quote above, that "life is beyond matter".

As Werner Gitt pointed out, "Transfer of information plays a fundamental role in all living organisms... and this information regulates all life processes and procreative functions." DNA is literally life's information store. Information (in-formation: big data, the matrix, wave function) rather than matter or energy is increasingly being thought of as fundamental to all, and that which determines all, including humans. Perhaps it is the original code set to run and to go on infinitely in the great unfolding, evolving and emerging. In some sense it is, to quote Tolle, "unconditional loving presence, the organising principle" that interprets the information and binds the atoms together which makes us and all things. Perfect oneness like energy or information cannot be lost or destroyed, it just changes form and intensity. Perfect oneness is never separate from its manifestations, but we have come to imagine it so.

Self-consciousness is awareness of information; in-formation coming into form, experience, and perception of "now" and "here" delivered through the senses and arising in mind and influenced by our selective memories and our selected visions, wishes or choices – and therefore a representation of what appears to be "out-there". But the "out-there" is clearly of our construction and not separate from us.

Self-consciousness and collective consciousness as conscious agents (see Hoffman p.136) are self-organising and emerging to higher and higher levels through interaction and participation with everything as it moves towards enlightenment. Consciousness has now reached a level where it has become aware of itself and its entanglement (also known as action at a distance[28] in quantum physics) with everything which can aid its continuing emergence to ever-higher levels (also see Al-Khalili quote p.132). As consciousness has become aware of itself in the human form, it suggests that it is humanity that will aid this development process, and more deeply understanding and embodying this process is our greatest opportunity to overcome our seemingly intractable current existential problems and challenges.

Consciousness creates matter and reality. Consciousness and other interactions [29] are fundamental (see Hoffman P.80) to everything; materially, mentally, socially among other things. Observance and interaction create reality; they collapse wave function. To be human is to recognise the power of creation vested in us.

Awesome; that's the only word that comes close to describing what it means to be human. To be alive when so much around us that we consider to be inert matter is teeming with life. To be conscious, to comprehend, to be aware, to create, to empathise, to show compassion, to love; awesome!

Mind

"Study of mind and consciousness [in general] through established scientific methods is often difficult due to the observed-observer dichotomy. The Cartesian approach of dualism considering the mind and matter as two diverse and unconnected entities has been questioned by oriental schools of Yoga and Vedanta as well as by the recent quantum theories of modern physics.

Freudian and Neo-Freudian schools based on the Cartesian model have been criticized by the humanistic schools which come much closer to the Vedanta approach of Unitarianism." *Indian Journal of Psychiatry January 2013.*

The attributes of our finite self-consciousness reflected and projected in mind include our thoughts, feelings, sensations, images, and perceptions that we project from our individual experiences and awareness. I have heard mind described as a screen upon which the self (self-awareness) projects what it takes as its objective finite reality as it appears through the attributes of the mind (awareness) and senses.

I prefer to think of mind metaphorically as an orb of light containing a hologram (which is perhaps a better fit with the non-duality definition) rather than having a screen and a projector, as I watch the attributes of my finite mind interacting with the infinite perfect oneness (Spirit) – yet knowing that I choose or determine the reality experienced. All that is in the mind is finite and therefore in some sense illusory but nonetheless real for us, although clearly transient.

Jung uses the word "ego" in a somewhat different way to my definition, to describe the "centre of the field of self-consciousness that contains our conscious awareness of existing and a continuing sense of personal [separate] identity. It is the organiser of our thoughts and intuitions, feelings, and sensations, and has access to memories that are not repressed. The ego is the bearer of personality and stands at the junction between the inner and outer worlds or as the bridge between "I" and "us" in order that we may come to fully experience them both better [or indeed experience them as one]". This sounds to me very much like mind, or indeed my "orb" concept.

We must assume behind
this force [the atom] is the
existence of a conscious
and intelligent mind.
This mind is the matrix
of all matter.

MAX PLANCK

Bound up with a deep
feeling in a superior mind
that reveals itself in the
world of experiences.

EINSTEIN

Thought, Thinking and Knowledge

Pure thoughts – those that are the most profound, sometimes referred to as "lightbulb" moments, inspiration (literally meaning "in spirit") or insight – are not an outcome of the thinking process or a function resulting from the finite mind, but rather arise in self-consciousness from perfect oneness through spirit. Pure thought "brings something from the unknown [infinite] into the world of the known [finite], who brings something from God into the world, who helps God to utter something" *Osho*.

Thoughts that are generated within the finite mind through the process of finite thinking are human constructs.

Thinking is always limited because it cannot embrace the infinite.

Thoughts are not always present; they come and go. Thoughts can dissolve. Thought within the individual mind makes perfect oneness through self-awareness appear as time, and perception makes it appear as space. It objectifies. The mind brings time and space out of perfect oneness, and into apparent existence. Whilst the finite mind perhaps cannot directly experience perfect oneness, it can become more aware of it, and know it better, through quieting the mind, again moving towards enlightenment.

Thinking is the system and a process that takes place within the finite mind, utilising thoughts created out of experience, awareness and information, which are generally directed to producing outcomes or knowledge.

The ability to perceive
or think differently is
more important than the
knowledge gained.

BOHM

The notion that human beings can, through thinking (objectivity, rationality, analysis, logic, separation, fragmentation, deconstruction, theorising, labelling and naming) reason themselves into a position of dominance and through a scientific belief of "knowing" and "predicting", thus creating knowledge of an outside, separate world, is indeed a powerful notion, but this kind of thinking is associated with an egocentric mind and anthropocentricism, and needs therefore to change.

Thinking is fundamental to all that human beings do. Just *think* about it for a moment. The vast majority of everything around us has been created through thinking, be it tangible, a representation or perception. The table upon which I write came from thinking i.e., the idea of a table; the house in which I live was designed through thinking and constructed through thinking; I think about my position in the world, and so on. But does the modern technological world provide us enough time to think, to think for ourselves, or is much of the "thinking" performed by technology, systems, process and cultures we have set up around it; is the thinking being done for us, and are we being overly accepting or even aware of it. Are we being indoctrinated and enslaved for the benefit of others?

A critical perspective on the system and process of thinking therefore seems valid if we are to gain a deeper understanding of what we are, why we are here, how to act and how to "perceive or think differently". Bohm has some interesting perspectives on thought and "thought as a system":

> "Once we make the critical (and false) assumption that thought and knowledge are not participating in our sense of reality [or indeed creating it], but only reporting on it, we are committed to a view that does not take into account the complex, unbroken processes that underlie the world as we experience it."

Bohm further contends that the body, emotions, and intellect can now be understood as an:

> "Unbroken field of mutually informing thought and that therefore we are compelled to see thought as a system – concrete as well as abstract, active as well as passive, collective as well as individual."

In a dialogue with Bohm reported in his book "thought as a system", two interesting questions and answers arose:

QUESTION

"Is there nothing that's limited and known, except through looking at it wrongly?

BOHM

Thought always provides limits [finite], which have relative validity. I'm suggesting you have two possibilities. One is to say that everything is limited, and knowledge could "get" it all. And the other is to say that knowledge cannot get it all [infinite]. People are trying to find out what the ultimate knowledge is.

Scientists thought they had it in the nineteenth century [where much of our socio-economic, business, and economic philosophy and culture emanates from] and then they said, "no it's not so". Today there is no sign that we have the final theory yet, although people are talking about the "theory of everything", which they hope to get. But you could say, first of all, that any knowledge we've ever had has been limited. Now that doesn't prove anything, but it makes one question.

Suppose even that physicists had finally found the theory of everything – the ultimate, final particles, which we'll call the "ultimons". And then it would just go on century after century. They would calculate in terms of ultimons, and everything would work out. But there would still be no proof that maybe in the next minute or next hour or day or century they wouldn't discover a limit to it all and it wouldn't work.

In other words, there is no way to *know* that you've got it. So, it's a poor strategy to assume it, because if you assume that you have the ultimate then you won't look for anything else, and therefore it will tend to trap you. You have no way of knowing that you have the ultimate. You may say something like "God told me", but then people could say "how do you know that"? You can't ever get absolute assurance that you have the ultimate knowledge, no matter how convinced you are of it. The best you can say is "as far as I can see, that's the way it is."

QUESTION

"Then the search for the ultimate in terms of knowledge might be a mistake in itself?

BOHM

Yes, it may be a very serious mistake – part of the flaw in the system [of thinking] we're talking about. We have to be open. Everything is changing every moment, and the possibility of keeping track of it is nil."

Intuitive knowledge is the highest level of knowledge, it involves… the entire process of life.

UNKNOWN

For if our sense of wonder were once to be awakened, we should no longer be able to act sacrilegiously.

KIM TAPLIN

Perhaps one of the greatest limiting aspects to our awareness, our experience, and our ability to communicate the impact that the infinite has on our being is language. As Lieberman comments "This [these] experience[s] could never be reduced to words". Therefore, words are inadequate to fully describe reality. Bohm argued that our language was far too object oriented, or noun based, and argued that this was making us see a world of static objects instead of dynamic processes.

Stedall has an interesting view on thought:
"If therefore my brain is not in itself the source of my thoughts and ideas but rather the organ, the filter through which this activity can express itself, what then is the actual nature and source of this activity we call mind and which on the whole we simply take for granted? And what is its relation to time?

Is this perhaps what some would call the human spirit; an entity that constantly interacts with the creative thoughts that animate the cosmos itself; thoughts that stem from a reality some would call God? Indeed, is the human spirit dynamic evidence of that reality itself?"

ELEMENT THREE

Signposts: feeling our way into the future. Learning to be on the right side of history.

MEMORANDUM FOR DISCUSSION

From: David Brook

To: God, the cosmos, our home planet Earth the whole of her ecology (including all living entities), down to every microbe, element, atom, subatomic particle, string, the macrocosm, and the microcosm.

Subject: Sorry for messing things up! Signposts towards a sustainable future and enlightenment for all.

Date: September 2022

Let me start by saying: I love you.

The quotation opposite from Krishnamurti, along with this quote from Rogers and Freiberg "If we are to preserve this fragile planet and build a future world of worthy whole persons capable of creating a sustainable and meaningful society then there can be no nobler pursuit than providing good education for our children [and adults], for without doubt they are responsible for creating the future" goes some way towards explaining why we are establishing our NOW Academy and Quantum Education and Development (QED). Quantum Education and Development embraces its Latin abbreviation "this is what was to be proved" and therefore by definition it is about life-long learning and life-long exploration. It is about the journey, not the destination – and it is integral.

A school is a place where one learns about the totality, the wholeness of life. Academic excellence is absolutely necessary, but a school includes much more than that. It is a place where both the teacher and the student explore, not only the outer world, the world of knowledge, but also their own thinking, their own behaviour.

KRISHNAMURTI

My heart rouses thinking to bring you news of something that concerns you and concerns many men [and women]. Look at what passes for the new. You will not find it there but in despised poems. It is difficult to get the news from poems yet men [and women] die miserably everyday for lack of what is found there.

WILLIAM CARLOS WILLIAMS

A school, in this sense, is literally any individual, group, organisation or place (including our home, planet Earth and the cosmos beyond), physical or virtual, where learning and development is enacted (a learning community), in an unending quest for understanding, transformation and enlightenment. It is the [r]evolution of self-consciousness to more subtle and higher levels.

One of my challenges of the past few months has been to try to articulate what Sustainable Humane Ecology (SHE), and Personal Venture (PV) elements mean, and to identify sources from which to draw upon and explore in order to establish processes through which the ultimate search for purpose and meaning toward an enrichment and enlightenment of one's being may be sought. I use the term 'elements' loosely, as they are non-dualistic and integral. It is not possible to consider one without the other, as it is through the microcosm that you experience the macrocosm (and vice versa), and we are seeking to operate at a subtler level, closer to spirit than normally experienced.

Those who know me well will have heard me many times before use the quote mentioned earlier from Goethe: "Tell a wise person, or else keep silent, because the mass man will mock it right away. I praise what is truly alive." I have been blessed to have had the wise counsel of some incredible people who have inspired and encouraged me in being able to start articulating what we mean by SHE/PV.

At the centre of all we do is "peace". There can be no other way than through peace, and peace is achieved through harmony, coherence, compassion, love and understanding; through removing all boundaries. I turn to Black Elk to illuminate when he speaks a profound truth:

Peace comes within the souls of men [and women]
When they realise their oneness with the universe.

BLACK ELK

106

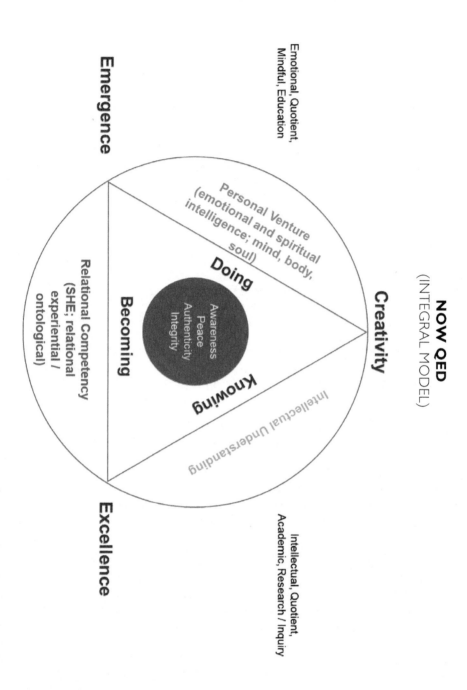

Emotional, Quotient,
Mindful, Education

Emergence

NOW QED
(INTEGRAL MODEL)

Personal Venture
(emotional and spiritual
intelligence; mind, body,
soul)

Doing

Creativity

Relational Competency
(SHE; relational
experiential /
ontological)

Becoming

Awareness
Peace
Authenticity
Integrity

Knowing

Intellectual Understanding

Excellence

Intellectual, Quotient,
Academic, Research / Inquiry

Introduction and background

ECONOMICS CAN ONLY EVER BE A SUBSET OF ECOLOGY.

We can express SHE/PV as a developmental, evolutionary and emergent process towards enlightenment, which is their main purpose, and as a solution to the current problem of separation, imposition of boundaries, fragmentation, illusion, materialism, inequality, over-consumption, greed, and an egocentric mindset.

Currently there is an urgency concerning matters of great importance surrounding our approach to our relationships – all our relationships, with the various aspects of ourselves, each other, our home planet Earth, and the cosmos – and it concerns all of us.

The root of our problems lies in issues associated with death, fear and an egocentric mindset that separates and seeks to control. Many psychologists contend that all fear is rooted in the fear of death or "non-being", "loss of life" and "annihilation". Interestingly, in Freud's view, nobody believes in their own death, so there is clearly a strong sense of denial. Indeed, this would appear to be the case with our wholly inappropriate response to the climate crisis and environmental degradation. It is death, or loss, separation – either actual or metaphorical – of ourselves (a form of suicide), along with our only means of survival – our home, planet Earth – and it is we who are killing her, by our own hands; for without us she would be thriving. One could say we are enacting our own human genocide or ecocide, which are crimes or sins against humanity, the cosmos and God. This is where fear sits: all fear

The party's over

It's [*not*] the economy,
stupid. (James Carville)
It's ecology, stupid.

We do not inherit the
world from our ancestors,
we borrow it from
our children.

NATIVE AMERICAN SAYING

arises from ignorance, lack of self-knowledge (of perfect oneness) and an egocentric mindset. Death is an illusion; it is but a transition from one state to another (taking off the headset see p.166). Our real problem is fear. As one awakens from the finite mind driven manifestations of separation that we are putting ourselves through, to the realisation of our infinite, perfect oneness (enlightenment) we can experience a sense of grief. This sense of grief is powerful and can be overwhelming as our established, ingrained way of life threatens all life on Earth.

Kubler-Ross identifies five stages of grief (described within this context) as:

Denial: it is not happening, the Earth will correct the situation, we have no other options, etc.

Anger: directed towards unmet expectations, self-imposed limits, towards "others", "the system", our ancestors or the vagaries of historical contexts.

Bargaining: for happiness with money, we earn in jobs we don't like, in order to buy stuff we don't need (which always end up in landfill), creating an endless cycle that can lead to...

Depression: the growing illness of our time, and then finally...

Acceptance: letting go and remembering what it means to be human.

The solutions broadly lie in the expansion of our humanity (compassion, tolerance, understanding, love, and care), sustainability (the property of systems to remain diverse and productive indefinitely), enlightenment (learning, intelligence, knowledge, wisdom, insight, education), and in the learning, development and evolution process, which is how we develop together; how we cohere and understand what we truly are.

As with all problems, the process by which solutions come to light lies within learning: learning to understand, learning to change, to grow and to develop, learning to *be* different, learning what it means to *be* part of this sacred experience we are having, and our greatest and perhaps only teacher is our environment.

Much of the modernist paradigm of the past few hundred years or so has been based on an anthropocentric, rational, objective, separate, egocentric mindset, ever-increasing economic growth and consumption, and the paradigms and cultures emanating therefrom. Indeed, there is an irony that as science and psychology pull increasingly toward infinite holism, our global culture is becoming predominantly more finite, separate and closed. It is lagging behind, as Eliot so eloquently put it:

> Endless invention, endless experiment,
> Brings knowledge of motion, but not of stillness;
> Knowledge of speech, but not of silence;
> Knowledge of words, and ignorance of the Word.
> All our knowledge brings us nearer to our ignorance,
> All our ignorance brings us nearer to God.
> Where is the Life we have lost in living?
> Where is the wisdom we have lost in knowledge?
> Where is the knowledge we have lost in information?
> The cycles of Heaven in twenty centuries
> Bring us farther from God and nearer to Dust.

Eliot would be amazed to see how right his words were, as our current dominant culture is awash with information, with sound bites through social media, with much of it false or fake; and seemingly, Google has an answer for everything. It is estimated that Americans spend almost five hours a day on their mobile devices and the Chinese over six, however for China the content is determined by the authoritarian regime as they do not allow access to 'outside' information or dialogue. But our knowledge and wisdom seem to be diminishing, with many searching to 'find' themselves in a quest for purpose and meaning. As we approach information overload, we increasingly become mesmerised by the speed and volume of text and images, not knowing what to believe. We can't see the wood for the trees.

What we need now is to recognise the integral nature of what we perceive as separate: minds, bodies and souls. Perhaps, for the benefit of our children and future generations, it is best to think about our engagement as through a community of souls.

SHE and PV programmes will be where we learn to truly understand what it means to be human beings, to *be* and *become*, where we explore, where we seek, where we strive, serve, love, and learn in and through mutual development – and through this developmental process, the solutions to our challenges will emerge. Perhaps the most important question that students of whatever age and disposition (all who are part of the NOW communities) can explore is 'how should one live this most precious and sacred life one has been given?'

The programmes sit at the heart of the NOW Academy culture, values and constitutions. They are part of our raison d'être. They differentiate us and they reflect the changes we consider necessary if we are to create a wholesome, sustainable, and coherent society - one that rises to the challenges resulting from the disastrous separation associated with much of human existence to date: all forms of inequality, globalisation, poverty, the climate crisis, pollution etc.

Some of the initial topics to be covered, expanded and added to include:

Exploring the human condition: consciousness, thinking, emotions, self, relationship, soul, spirit, communication, play, creativity, culture, tolerance, compassion, ethics, storytelling, purpose...

21st-Century life: historic perspectives, globalisation, inequality, climate crisis, geopolitics, corporate capitalism, economics, information, knowledge, social media, stewardship, citizenship, technological development, making a living, business...

Ecology and environment: systems theory, organisation, deep ecology, sustainability, life, cosmology, biodiversity, emergence theory, society...

The quantum age: context and perspective, no boundary, determining reality, chaos and complexity, time & space, creating the future, infinite potential, indeterminacy, artificial intelligence, wholeness...

Frameworks: philosophical, psychological, scientific, sociological, ecological, an introduction to action research methodology...

Personal mastery: identifying and developing gifts, nurturing talent, developing ecovisionery leadership, mindfulness, realising our potential, becoming who we are meant to be...

We believe that each person is born into the world for a purpose, bearing unique gifts that unfold over one's lifetime, therefore to "know thyself and to be thyself" is the highest achievement one can attain in this life. These programmes, along with our overall experiences, both individually and collectively, represent the pathways and guides to such attainment. A quote from Socrates illuminates:

"The unexamined life is not worth living."

What I believe Socrates is alluding to here is that only through striving to know and understand ourselves, by "examining" ourselves and our lives – both individually and collectively – can our lives have any meaning. Our programmes provide the frameworks, time and space for such striving to be enacted.

And NOW Academy programmes are here to help you find out why.

A poetic insight and three relevant quotes illuminate further:

> You must learn one thing.
> The world was made to be free in.
> Give up all other worlds
> except the one to which you belong.
> Anything or anyone
> that does not bring you alive
> is too small for you.
> **Whyte**

"The most important days in your life are the day you are born and the day you find out why."
MARK TWAIN

"The privilege of a lifetime is to become who we truly are."
JUNG

"May you experience each day as a sacred gift, woven around the heart of wonder."
O'DONOHUE

Much about the human condition is to do with finding our way, both in and through the world, and the cosmos beyond. In many ways, we are explorers and adventurers: materially, philosophically, psychologically, and theologically. Some of the biggest open questions are those to do with our position in the world: sustainability, purpose, meaning, life, and death.

A culture that alienates
itself from the very ground
of its own being - from
the wilderness (nature and
ecosystem) outside and
from that other wilderness
within – is doomed to very
destructive behaviour,
ultimately perhaps
self-destructive
behaviour.

GARY SNYDER

The separateness (religions, cultures, ideologies, inequality) that alienated us from each other and our environment through the anthropocentric culture of the 19th, 20th and early 21st centuries, could easily be described as "self-destructive".

Some of the major rifts of separation that aided our current catastrophic situation and need our urgent and immediate attention are:

- The perceived separation between humankind and Earth
- The separation we have imposed between nation states
- The separation we have imposed between virtue and business
- The perceived separation of mind, body, and soul
- The perceived separation between different religions
- The perceived separation between matter and energy

The first step towards uniting starts with recognising the wholeness that surrounds us and from which we are made manifest, of which we are a reflection and vice versa. Indeed, whilst it is useful to describe the rifts above, they are just reflections of the greater whole. They are all integral, and as we move our attention towards healing elements of one, it will also help us heal elements of the others.

SHE/PV programmes are, by their very nature, inextricably interlinked, both to each other and to our overall QED model – as are students, mentors and teachers, with any participant capable of playing each and every role. Our challenge is not only to find ways of teaching, guiding and mentoring these programmes, but also to embody them ourselves through our behaviour as we all learn and lead through example.

It is therefore vital that we clearly communicate to those interested in becoming involved with us that they must fully embody the culture and ethos of NOW, SHE and PV. We need to have some form of initial collective understanding of this evidenced, and to have an ongoing programme of personal development and action research underpinning it. In other words, we will need to have an internal programme similar to those we are delivering within the NOW Academy. We will need to become a true learning community – sharing inspirations, exchanging thoughts, consciousness, experiences and insights – and learning that we are in this together. We do not draw a distinction between the NOW community and the others, and this is the core of oneness. There is no "us and them", there is only a "we" the very core.

Sustainable Humane Ecology

SHE; because we are all in this together, there is no other way; NOW.

SHE will seek to continuously reflect and question through applying a critical perspective (and in dialogue with a broad and diverse audience) to the initial perspectives contained herein, in order to clarify, expand and evolve its emergent content and its application, to ensure its validity and that it does not turn into static dogma.

Firstly, we are seeking to challenge, and where appropriate, reset the initial and essential assumptions upon which much of human culture currently rests in order to enable us to become more humane and sustainable. This will provide something of a wrapper, guiding principles and a backdrop to what will follow.

There is an academic body of work from which the SHE philosophy and methodology has been initially drawn and is being developed, called Human Ecology, as distinct from our humane ecology (see definitions below). Some leading institutions on the subject are Cornell University, University of Kent, and Lund University. Definitions of human ecology include:

ENCYCLOPEDIA.COM

"Human ecology is a way of looking at the interactions of humans with their environments and considering this relationship as a system. In this theoretical framework, biological, social, and physical aspects of the organism are considered within the context of their environments."

Man was (is) to learn from nature (cosmos) rather than subdue it.

TAPLIN

WIKIPEDIA

"Human ecology is an interdisciplinary and transdisciplinary study of the relationship between humans and their natural, social, and built environments."

NOW ACADEMY

We all need to study human ecology because we need to understand our relationship with other human beings and with the complex environments in which we exist, from the different spaces that humankind has built and the multitude of societies and cultures that inhabit them, and the nature that surrounds us and our planet, to the virtual world of technology and beyond.

SHE represents an adaptive and emergent philosophical framework and process within which to explore "what it means to be human"; it is a core element in our QED model, and whilst there is specific content to be explored and research undertaken from within each discrete segment, by its very nature SHE also embraces the whole model.

The content herein represents our initial identification of points for further development of the subject matter for SHE, where – it is worth repeating – the meaning ascribed to each letter is:

SUSTAINABLE

"Development that meets the needs of the present without compromising the ability of future generations to meet their own needs" (World Commission on Environment and Development, 1987). In this definition, "needs" are material, ecological, emotional, social, and spiritual. But it is also a little more complex than this, because "Development, as a concept, has been associated with diverse meanings, interpretations, and theories from various scholars. Development is defined as 'an evolutionary process in which the human capacity increases in terms of initiating new structures, coping with problems, adapting to continuous change, and striving purposefully and creatively to attain new goals (Peet, 1999 cited in Du Pisani, 2006). According to Reyes (2001), development is understood as a social condition within a nation, in which the needs of its population are satisfied by the rational and sustainable use of natural resources and systems. Todaro and Smith (2006) also define development as a multi-dimensional process that involves major changes in social structures, attitudes, and institutions, as well as economic growth, reduction of inequality, and eradication of absolute poverty. Several theories have been put forward to explain the concept of development. They include the theories of Modernisation, Dependency, World Systems and Globalisation".[30]

HUMANE

Humane (humanity, humanities): compassionate, understanding, tolerant, kind, loving, philanthropic, alleviation of suffering, to do as little harm as possible. Stanford University describes the humanities as "The study of how people process and document the human experience." Professor David Behling describes the humanities as: "Finding answers to this question "what does being human mean?. The humanities reveal many different kinds of people and ways of thinking about life, the universe and everything."

ECOLOGY

Ecology: from Greek meaning "The study of the relationship between living things and their environments" also associated here with Gaia Goddess Mother Earth. Currently, in respect of our relationship with Gaia, it is at a low ebb, seen in environmental degradation and the climate crisis, and it needs to be healed. We need to move from poverty and gross inequality (death and decay) to sustainable prosperity (thriving and growth).

Fundamentally, SHE is about our relationship with our home, our "Mother Earth", from whom we have all been born and to whom we shall all return.

In uttering the words 'sustainable humane ecology', we start to take an important yet tentative step towards knowing our "self". We recognise that through a better understanding of what we perceive as the "other", and by being seen and known for who and what we are by the "other" (both human and non-human) – emanating from an unbounded, creative, open systems paradigm – we better understand our "self". We also come to recognise that this "self" is inextricably inter-related to all other "selves", both human and non-human – you don't love your neighbour as your "self", you love them because they are you. A course in Miracles explains lesson 196 "It can be but myself I crucify. When this is firmly understood and kept in full awareness you will not attempt to harm yourself, nor make your body a slave to vengeance. You will not attack yourself, and you will realise that to attack another is but to attack yourself. You will be free of the insane belief that to attack a brother saves yourself. And you will understand his safety is your own, and in his healing, you are healed. Such is the form of madness you believe, if you accept

119

the fearful thought, you can attack another and be free yourself". Osho put it another way when he said that "Love is the experience of oneness".

Indeed, it is love which is the guiding theme running throughout SHE, and it is love which is the force leading us towards enlightenment through emancipation. When you look for the "I", what you find is relating; you find "us", bound in, through and by love, and love is the energy determining the quality of relationship.

This is the quest for SHE: to engage in heartfelt connection with all that surrounds us as we move towards a deeper and higher communion with everything through a [r]evolution in self-consciousness, not only to repair the damage done but to stop further damage being done through an egocentric mindset, and to evolve an emergent society founded upon an altruistic mindfulness[31] moving ever forwards towards enlightenment.

> "The illusion of separateness we create in order to utter the words
> "I am" is part of our problem in the modern world. We have
> always been far more a part of great patterns on the globe than
> our fearful egos can tolerate knowing... To preserve nature is to
> preserve the matrix through which we can experience our souls
> and the soul of the planet."
> *Walter Christie*

We exist through and within a complex matrix that connects all.

In 1975, physicist Henry Stapp (in a US federal report) postulated that "Everything in the universe is connected as an indivisible whole", and experiments based on Bell's Theorem[32] have shown this to be true, namely that reality is non-local and non-dualistic.

What's there to be frightened of when we are connected to everything? It's only the separate self that can fear others that, in reality, don't exist.

We need to wake up from the "illusion of separateness" and the egocentric mind, which is currently the dominant global paradigm, and recognise that the human soul and the planetary (cosmic) soul are one holomovement[33] flowing through the "matrix". In doing harm to our planet or "others", through separation and an egocentric mind, we are harming ourselves along with all "others".

Everything is connected to and affecting everything else all the time. It is not possible to "separate" except through looking at 'things' wrongly, and through deceiving ourselves from within an egocentric mind. We cannot have any losers; if one or other of us loses, or our planet loses, then the matrix loses, and we all lose.

"...the ego seems to maintain clear and sharp lines of
demarcation. There is only one state – admittedly an unusual
state, but not one that can be stigmatised as pathological – in
which it does not do this. At the height of being in love, the
boundary between ego and object threatens to melt away. Against
all the evidence of the senses, a person in love declares the "I"
and "you" are one and is prepared to behave as if it were a fact."
Freud

In this respect, the ego (a person's sense of self-importance as a separate being in their outside world) is a boundary to achieving unconditional love for oneself in the first instance, and then towards others, both human and non-human. From a SHE/PV perspective, unconditional love is a prerequisite if we are truly to remove all the boundaries (imposed by an egocentric mindset) to the heartfelt connection with others that's necessary to create a truly sustainable and prosperous future. More on this vital energy, love, is to come in element Four.

"It is obvious to me that the forests [the starving, the oceans,
poverty, inequality etc.] cannot be saved one at a time: without a
profound revolution [or re-evolution returning to evolution] in
human consciousness."
Theodore Roszak

Whilst SHE/PV draws upon content from all other theories, disciplines and subjects, in both the sciences and humanities, it goes beyond intellect. It is a process and a practice by which the revolution in human self-consciousness from the egocentric mind to altruistic mindfulness – from illusion to reality, from fear to unconditional love, and from separateness to wholeness – is enacted and embodied.

SHE is about adaptive, emerging, open, dynamic systems; not about discrete, closed, finite systems, such as globalisation run on predatory competitive lines of continuing and increasing consumption, with winners and losers.

"The consumer society fails to deliver on its promise of fulfilment
through material comforts because human wants are insatiable,
human needs are socially defined, and the real sources of
personal happiness are elsewhere. Indeed, the strength of social
relations and the quality of leisure – both crucial psychological
determinants of happiness in life – appear as much diminished

as enhanced in the consumer class. The consumer society, it
seems, has impoverished people by raising their incomes."
Alan Durning

The consumer society to which Durning refers, through its materialism and creation of insatiable wants, which by definition can never be satisfied, produces a totally unsustainable and pathogenic global culture, and is the antithesis of SHE/PV.

SHE
Perspectives

To further illuminate and provide deeper insight about the need (or the case) for SHE, I have viewed it from a number of different perspectives, drawing on some eminent thinkers (the "giants" mentioned earlier) in their respective fields of expertise. Without the contribution of their insights and inspiration, the concept of SHE would not have emerged. I have not elaborated too much on the quotes as their words speak powerfully for themselves, but we will want to engage in dialogue around them further as we progress. Whilst I have used a variety of quotes, I considered it necessary to produce a richness of deeper understanding and potential for learning about the work we are undertaking, in order to ensure that those wishing to join us can make an informed decision – and I am sure they are worthy of your close consideration and further investigation and exploration.

PROBLEM PERSPECTIVE

"Although my eyes were open, they might just as well've been closed."
Procol Harum

"We now live chiefly by the mind, as separate individuals
acting on and relating to other separate individuals and on a
lifeless, dumb world beyond the body. Applying our mind to the
matter [dualistic observance] around us, we have produced an
extraordinary material culture."
David Suzuki

"To be identified with your mind is to be trapped in time: the compulsion to live almost exclusively through memory and anticipation. This creates an endless preoccupation with past and future and an unwillingness to honour and acknowledge the present moment and allow it to be."
Tolle

"Once we make the critical (and false) assumption that thought and knowledge are not participating in our sense of reality, but only reporting on it, we are committed to a view that does not take into account the complex, unbroken processes that underlie the world as we experience it."
Bohm

"Ahriman is an evil spirit, his essential nature is expressed through his principal epithet "the lie" expressed as greed, wrath, and envy. He is the calculating manipulator who tries not to seduce like Lucifer but to enslave individual man to make him part of a collective to let him forget his cosmic origins to chain him to a lifeless Earth."
Rudi Lissau

"We owe our rationality and earthly know-how to the influence of Ahriman, but it is an influence that has led us, among other things, to believe only what can be weighed and measured, and to experience of what Tarnas calls the "disenchanted cosmos", a view which empowers the utilitarian mindset."
Stedall

"The world we have created is an extraordinary, unprecedented achievement, constructed out of the awesome power of our abstracting, pattern making brain. But it has lacked the ingredient we discover we depend on to thrive - the idea of wholeness and connection we call spirit. Our cultural narrative [global] does not include these [spiritual] beliefs... the consequences (of which) are threatening indeed - the negation of being."
Suzuki

"Unity and common purpose are corrupted by capitalism. Nothing is to be had for money except mediocrity, as Schopenhauer admirably said. Capitalism and representative democracy invariably lead to corruption."
Gesswein

"From my experience, trying to engage in philosophy as a means to improving awareness and understanding on a day-by day basis has been extremely fraught. Mainly it would appear that the vast majority of people are simply too prepared to accept the dogma inherited from history, their indoctrination and the rhetoric emanating from The System. It is as if they are lost in a fog, as if mesmerised by the allure of the promises they have been made. They either treat the subject as anathema or debunk it on the grounds that it raises such mega questions that are impossible to answer."
Peter Anthony

"We are in between two stories right now and are in need of a new one.".
Unknown

In his writing "The Circle of Atonement", Robert Perry comments on the "Little Hindrance" taken from *A Course in Miracles*: "the separation, the single error of separation [from what once was whole]: the choice of separateness over oneness: of death over life" and "this error fragmented into billions of separate situations and events, as if this one error was seen refracted in a kaleidoscope. Each situation and event was a fractured version of the original error." It was an error of selfish individuation.

This error was implicitly taken up by Adam Smith when he postulated that "self-interest" and "the minimum and essential individualism which can be assured to be present in all men..." was the "mainspring" (note the mechanical metaphor) of the capitalist economic system. Such a system advanced through unfettered consumption, and the quest for constant economic growth and globalisation has compounded the "error" and the "lie" (see Ruskin's lie and Anthony's damned lie below) to a point where the human and non-human worlds have become unsustainable and unstable. Both of these were further compounded by the notion of the selfish gene postulated by Richard Dawkins. So, from NOW's perspective, Perry's "error of separation", Smith's error of "essential individualism", the "lie" and Dawkins "selfish gene" need to be corrected along the lines identified in Element Two and SHE/PV, as they are all essentially wrong. Indeed, in the time since Smith's and Dawkins' assertions, there is much evidence from mainstream psychology and science to refute such claims, having proven the holistic, interconnected, and cooperative basis of everything, many of which are included herein.

In a paper written by Professor Peter Antony entitled "Economics: The damned lie", he comments:

Every aspect of life
has been absorbed into
the commercial-industrial
context. We seem not
to know how to live
in any other way.

BERRY

"John Ruskin in 'Unto This Last' published in 1859 commenting on the prevailing economic doctrine pronounces in violent terms; "a lie - wholly and to the very root - the so-called science [Smith's economics] is the most cretinous, speechless, paralyzing plague…" The doctrine, inherited in a vulgarised version from Adam Smith's 'An Inquiry into the Nature and Causes of the Wealth of Nations' (1776), set out to establish that the unfettered relationship of market competition was the best if not the only means of determining production and demand by the prevailing and beneficent influence of self-interest. Ruskin believed this to be a false doctrine because it rested on an abstraction of the most selfish human characteristics which were then magnified to dominant proportions and finally made into a model for general imitation. The result is a monstrous caricature held up for our approval. The so-called science is contrary to all traditional, religious, and moral teaching and opposed by every decent precept of social relationships.

Generally speaking, we respect soldiers, doctors, and priests because we believe that in due circumstances, they will be prepared to die for the duty imposed in their work. The very idea is laughable in the case of merchants because we presume them to act selfishly. A society which has embraced economic doctrine has made that presumption of selfishness into a moral duty."

In a similar vein Berry comments: "So influential is the present commercial-industrial order that our dominant professions and institutions are functioning in this context; not merely economics, but government, jurisprudence, the medical profession, religion and education. Every aspect of life has been absorbed into the commercial-industrial context. We seem not to know how to live in any other way."

In some sense, we are now living out an old story founded upon a lie: *predatory capitalist competition* that delivers inequality, insatiable *consumption* that destroys the planet, *separation* that creates conflict, *materialism* that negates our essential nature and engenders power and control, and the *lie* that – if we pledge allegiance to the system that supports the foregoing – we may one day attain dominance and join the elites. It is a violation against our children and humanity to continue to sell such a false promise, and to promulgate the *error*.

SOLUTION PERSPECTIVE

Many of the problems and challenges we face are existential, and they apply to our whole ecological system. These problems and challenges are solely humankind's responsibility; we created them, and we can solve them. The solutions will require radical and fundamental changes to our behaviour, self, collective consciousness, mindset, and culture on all levels – individual, corporate, organisational and political – and will require a fundamental, deep and unifying shift in our understanding of what it means to be human.

Identifying where the solutions lie will be our first and most urgent priority, and implementing the changes is likely to require lifelong and generational actions, both individually and collectively. Gandhi once said, "Be the change you want to see in the world", and the changes required will first have to be transformational at the individual level (we need to remember our destiny) before they can emanate throughout all of society, as society (with all its sub-cultures) is a human construct, and must authentically reflect our fundamental, philanthropic, holistic nature. Some initial signposts as to where solutions may be found are encapsulated in the following quotes:

"There is no reality except the one contained within us.
That is why so many people live such an unreal life. They take the images outside them for reality and never allow the world within to assert itself."
Herman Hesse

"We need to move from separateness and fragmentation to wholeness through a greater degree of consciousness, both individually and collectively."
Stedall

"When awake, we experience everything as outside ourselves and as separate – we look outwards. In sleep we enter into quite another relationship with the world and with the surrounding universe – and even more so I suspect when we are no longer inhabiting a physical body – then we look inwards. What was outside becomes our inner experience. In other words, we become the object itself.

We no longer experience our separateness. We become in Steiner's words a 'macrocosmic' being ... the universe becomes our organism. Humanities waking life can be compared to a prison, yet when asleep or between incarnations, like a release

from prison. Imagine not being the observer of spring but being spring itself."
Stedall

"If mind and matter are ultimately as inseparable as matter and energy in quantum physics, then there is only one reality - a reality that Schumacher saw in human beings; a reality that is three quarters hidden but hidden only if we 'look' rather than 'see'. Three quarters hidden and not accessible to objective, scientific observation! We need far more intelligence to 'see' rather than scientific 'looking'."
Stedall

"What we now want is closer contact and better understanding between individuals and communities all over the Earth, and the elimination of egoism and pride which is always prone to plunge the world into primeval barbarism and strife... Peace can only come as a natural consequence of universal enlightenment."
Tesla

"Perhaps the greatest obstacle of all is certainty – another form of laziness which cuts us off from further exploration. Only the closed mind is certain."
Stedall

"For those at one with the Oneness, everything is good."
Taoist saying

May we all wake up.
May we all become enlightened.
May Mother Earth come back into balance.
May we all heal – physically, emotionally,
spiritually and on a planetary level.
May love become our religion.
Mia Genis

NEW SCIENTIFIC (QUANTUM) PERSPECTIVE

Quantum mechanics, along with the broader quantum phenomenon and metaphor, has had, and is increasingly having, a major impact on our lives. Quantum technology has brought us our 'smart' communication devices – the phones, tablets, and laptops that have enabled the information, social media and communications revolutions – along with MRI scanners, lasers, atomic clocks, GPS and LED screens. The advent of quantum computers along with artificial intelligence and robotics promises further revolutionary leaps into the future, perhaps even questioning the human role in "doing" anything, and thereby further releasing and fuelling human beings to concentrate on their innate, imaginative, intuitive capacity for creativity and "being" – especially in support of both SHE and the critical need for a new form of learning, education and personal/social development, such as that proposed herein.

Quantum physics has changed the way we need to think about reality, as: "You can ask the physicists about this; do they actually think that physical objects exist and have specific properties like position, momentum and spin when they're not observed and the technical question asked is; is local realism true? Realism means that properties like position, momentum and spin, even when they're not observed, do they have definite values, and locality means that they have influences that propagate no faster than the speed of light and we have tested whether local realism is true over and over again and it turns out that it's false [it turns out that unless they are observed, measured physical objects do not exists in a specific time and space]. Local realism is false and something else called non-contextual realism, the idea, do particles have their position, momentum and spin, definitive values, and do the values they have not depend on how we measure them, that's the non-contextual, and it turns out non-contextual realism, the claim that they have their values, and the values are definitive and don't depend on how we measure them that's also false.

From the physicist's point of view the idea that there is a distinction between the classical point of view and the quantum world which was called part of the Copenhagen Interpretation has really fallen into disfavour recently what physicists are finding is that they can get quantum effects from billions of atoms, we're getting almost like physical stuff here they're almost at the size of blood cells and so forth. In other words, the real physics from the physicists' point of view is quantum physics and the idea of classical physics being something separate from that is an old interpretation which I think not too many people hold anymore".
Hoffman.

Quantum physics has changed the way we need to think about reality.

HOFFMAN

"Quantum mechanics allows us to know how it [everything] interacts and how it all fits together, but it comes at a large price, at its fundamental level we have to accept that nature is ruled by chance and probability.

Atoms present us with dizzying contradictions. They can be both particles [matter] and waves [energy], and they can appear to be in more than one place at the same time. They force us to rethink what we mean by past and future, by cause and effect, and they tell us strange things about where the universe came from and where it's going – which is pretty amazing stuff for something that's just a millionth of a millimetre across. That's why Niels Bohr, the father of atomic physics said "when it comes to atoms, language can only be used as poetry [metaphor and abstract]."

Although we know how a single atom or just a few atoms behave, the way trillions of them come together in concert to create the world around us is still largely a mystery. The atoms that make up my body are identical to the atoms in the rocks and the trees, the air, and even the stars – and yet they come together to create a conscious being who can ask the question, what is an atom?"
Al-Khalili

The following is an extract, slightly paraphrased from an Alan Wallace video.

"What kinds of question are we posing to nature and how do we seek to get answers from them?

There are multiple stories [representations of what lies behind and what determines reality] to be told, and to listen to diverse ones that may be complementary or which may challenge our assumptions is an inherently worthwhile thing to do. "What we attend to is what we take to be real and what we don't attend to fades out", William James.

Quoting Sir Roger Penrose looking at the laws of nature and seeing how extraordinary mathematical they are: Why should that be the case? Maybe the underlying reality is not particles at all. Maybe it's forces (see Tesla p.78), maybe it is a dimension that is purely mathematical, and out of that emerges this world that we are experiencing, the world of nature.

It turns out there are fundamental constants throughout nature, throughout the universe, sets that had they been even slightly different, the universe would have been devoid of intelligent life, which led some very good physicists such as John Barrow, Frank Tipler and others to suggest that "There exists one possible universe designed with the goal of generating and sustaining observers", and that "Intelligent information processing must come into existence in the universe and once it comes into existence it will never die out (see the anthropic principle, p.21, and Schopenhauer contingency, p.21)."

In other words, the universe is life-friendly. There may be something like a life force that created this universe a stage for intelligent life; a house brought forth to contain everything within it.

Max Planck and Einstein suggest that maybe it's mind [consciousness, perfect oneness] that is the matrix of all matter behind the force of atoms; that there exists a conscious intelligent mind, and intelligent design. Einstein says, "There is a superior mind that reveals itself through the world of experience." James Jeans says, "The universe begins to look more like a giant thought rather than a giant machine". Mind no longer appears to be an accidental intruder in the realm of matter. We ought, rather, to hail it as the creator of the realm of matter. So, *what underlies what*, is both fundamental and crucial.

Wallace comments on the work of Wheeler, saying that "Semantic information, meaningful information, is fundamental. Underlying, and out of our concepts of information we create the constructs of particles, forces, space, time, matter, subject, and object and so on. Information is underlying, information is primary [all is in-formation]" (also see Gitt on p.93).

According to Andrei Linde, "This model of material world obeying laws of physics is so successful that soon we forget about our starting point and say that matter is the only reality, and perceptions are only helpful for its description... But in fact, we are substituting reality of our feelings by a successfully working theory of an independently existing material world... Is it possible that consciousness, like space-time, has its own intrinsic degrees of freedom, and that neglecting these will lead to a description of the universe that is fundamentally incomplete? What if our perceptions, what if consciousness is as real (or maybe, in a certain sense, are even more real) than material objects?" So, the core theory may be incomplete after all because something's left out: consciousness."

Here I slightly paraphrase content from Dr Stuart Hameroff's YouTube video: "In the quantum world, there is no flow of time. Time and the flow of time only exist in human consciousness. Only *now* exists, eternal; time is a human construct. We connect all the *nows* in sequence through memory. I use Sir Roger Penrose's definition "A particular type of collapse of wave function". In the quantum world, things can be in a superposition (multiple possible states, multiple possibilities) whose wave function can collapse into classical reality. Four identified ways in which wave function or superposition may collapse into classical reality are:

1. Conscious observation: the Copenhagen interpretation.[34]
2. Every superposition branches off and forms a new universe: multiple worlds hypothesis.

Our brain has
40 conscious events or
more per second.

3. Interaction of the superposition with the environment: quantum decoherance.[35]

4. Superpositions grow until they meet some kind of natural threshold inherent in nature, which causes the superposition to collapse into the classical state.

Penrose postulates that superposition is a separation in fundamental reality at the most basic level. The universe separates, and these separations are bubbles in reality. They are unstable and will collapse into one state or another. This is known as objective reduction, which is consciousness.

In the brain, it is thought that quantum computations (collapse) happen at about 40 times per second. But this is not to say this is the only way superposition collapses [see numbered list above]. Any superposition that reaches the threshold for collapse would have a degree of quantum consciousness. Some argue that the universe literally had a conscious moment during the big bang, and that our consciousness, indeed all consciousness, may be related to that initial conscious moment, so a degree of consciousness exists in everything.

Protoconsciousness (a state which precedes consciousness and can develop and maintain higher order consciousness) exists everywhere at the Planck scale.[36] Protoconsciousness is basically anything that is in superposition. Anything that is in superposition can become conscious if it avoids quantum decoherance and is allowed to evolve long enough to reach this threshold for self-collapse.

For a very large superposition, the larger it is, the harder it is to isolate from the environment to avoid decoherance, and the faster it will reach the threshold. So, an electron could reach the threshold if it were protected for 10 million years. Something larger, like a nanogram of protein in our brain, can reach the threshold in 25 milliseconds, which is roughly 40 conscious events per second or higher.

Do we create our reality? The extreme view would be that consciousness is all that there is, but that runs into the problem of solipsism.[37] Another possibility is that the Copenhagen interpretation says we create our reality by our observation; it collapses the wave function. The problem with that is it doesn't say what consciousness is, or why our brain is different to any other measuring device. It kind of puts consciousness outside science. So, my view is somewhere in the middle, like the Penrose objective reduction, where the superposition reaches the threshold, self-collapses and chooses a reality. At that point, it's kind of a multiple choice from multiple possibilities for each specific collapse, but the beauty is – according to Penrose – that Planktonic information embedded in the fundamental level of the universe helps to choose or influence which choice is made. The quantum information embedded at the Planck scale will influence your decision one way or another, for the good, generally. So, in some kind of way, it brings in divine guidance.

What happens to our consciousness when we die? While the brain is functioning, metabolism is occurring. Quantum coherence is being driven by metabolism. When that ends, when the blood supply stops flowing, quantum information leaks out into the universe at large because it exists at the Planck scale; it exists at the most fundamental level. When the quantum coherence is lost (when we die) it kind of leaks out but doesn't dissipate entirely because of entanglement and because the universe is probably holographic, so it remains in a phase relationship, and can persist at least at the subconscious dream-like state outside the body."

"What exists in the objective world, independent of my perceptions, is a world of conscious agents, not a world of unconscious particles and fields. ... Consciousness is fundamental."
Hoffman

"We are essentially blind to what exists at the very core of physical reality."
Marcelo Gliser

"In quantum theory we never end up with "things"; we always deal with interconnections... a complex web of relationships between the various parts of a unified whole. The realisation that systems are integrated wholes that cannot be understood by analysis."
Fritjof Capra

"Quantum physics tells us that nothing that is observed is unaffected by the observer. That statement, from science, holds an enormous and powerful insight. It means that everyone sees a different truth because everyone is creating what they see."
Neale Donald Walsch

"On this stream, one may see an ever-changing pattern of vortices, ripples, waves, splashes, etc., which evidently have no independent existence as such. Rather, they are abstracted from the flowing movement, arising and vanishing in the total process of the flow. Such transitory subsistence as may be possessed by these abstracted forms implies only a relative independence

or autonomy of behaviour, rather than absolutely independent existence as ultimate substances."
Bohm

"How often do they strive to divide that which, despite everything, would always remain single and whole?"
Goethe

"The vital act is the act of participation. "Participator" is the incontrovertible new concept given by quantum mechanics. It strikes down the term "observer" of classical theory, the one who stands safely behind the thick glass wall and watches what goes on without taking part. It can't be done, quantum mechanics says."
Wheeler

"We have to conclude that the old-style Newtonian universe is an illusion, for there is no such thing as an external world 'out there' that exists from consciousness. Everything is mind. We are not part of the universe; we are the universe."
Andrew Powell

"Everything is process all the way 'down' and all the way 'up', and processes are irreducibly relational – they exist only in patterns, networks, organisations, configurations, or webs. In the process view, 'up' and 'down' are context-relative terms used to describe phenomena of various scales and complexity. There is no base level of elementary entities to serve as the ultimate 'emergent base' on which to ground everything.

Phenomena at all scales are not entities but relatively stable processes, and since processes achieve stability at different levels of complexity, while still interacting with processes at other levels, all are equally real, and none has absolute ontological primacy."
Evan Thomson

"The separation of matter and spirit is an abstraction.
The ground is always one."
Jakob Bohme

The ramifications of our understanding of reality and the materialist perspective are profound, and they offer a deep insight as to how humankind might be able to overcome its existential threats and participate in a truly sustainable manner.

"I am puzzled about the manner in which the individual himself influences the observations which he believes are telling him the truth about nature and the universe."
Bernard Lovell

"I have become aware of what Jung has called "the noumenal reality which embraces the whole situation", which includes the observer and the observed."
Watson

"The observer and the observed are in their innermost essence one and the same thing."
Stedall

"Something much deeper is resurfacing in the emerging consciousness of our time, namely, we are our relationships."
O'Murchu

"Fields can be understood as horizons of belonging, creating a relational matrix for creative possibilities... they are fundamentally a process of becoming."
Lovell

"Learn how to see. Realise that everything connects to everything else."
Leonardo DaVinci

ECOLOGICAL PERSPECTIVE

An ecological perspective by its very nature is that of an open system where everything has an impact on and relies to a greater or lesser extent on everything else "all the way down and all the way up" (see Thomson p.137). It is a truly holistic perspective.

Unfortunately, much of the narrative surrounding humankind's take on an ecological perspective has been one of dualism and denial, separating itself from all the other aspects, setting itself in dominion over them. It studies, exploits and treats them as insignificant and subject to its own ends, and in doing so, has ignored that it is but an element of the process and needs the flourishing of the whole in order to survive. This narrow focus has produced an existential threat to all life, a form of ecocide, genocide and suicide of ourselves and our home, planet Earth, and is sacrilegious by any measure.

The impact humankind is having on the Earth and its population (environmental degradation, species extinction, global warming, to name but a few) may seem irrelevant for a society dominated by a pathogenic system and an elite (e.g., the Trump era, right wing populism, and China and Russia's totalitarianism, and the wealthy elites) wedded to actions and objectives (e.g., continuous GDP growth increasing personal and state capital and hedonism through increasing consumption) that deny there is a fundamental and existential problem between closed and open (ecological) systems.

Sir David Attenborough, in the Netflix programme *A Life on Our Planet*, provides a useful and definitive summary, which I slightly paraphrase here:

"Summer sea ice has reduced by 40% in the last forty years; our planet is losing its ice. Global warming is at a speed of change greater than any of the last ten thousand years. Human Beings have overrun the world. It is a story of global decline in a single generation with only 35% of wilderness remaining in 2019 when compared to the start of my generation. We cut down over 50 billion trees each year and wild animal populations have halved since the 1950s.

Humans account for 30% of the weight of mammals with the next 60% for the animals we eat, so 90% in all for humans. This is now our planet: run by humankind. There is little left for the rest of the living world. Humankind's blind assault on the planet has finally come to alter the very fundamentals of the living world."

"Love Nature as much as possible, it is the best drug of all."
Gesswein

"Ultimately, Deep Ecological awareness is spiritual... human spirit is understood as the mode of consciousness in which the individual feels a sense of belonging, of connectedness, to the cosmos as a whole... Deep Ecological awareness is spiritual in its deepest essence... it is consistent with the "perennial philosophy" of Christian mystics, Buddhists, or native American Indians."
Naess

"Until you're right with the earth, nothing can prosper and there's nothing to celebrate."
Ron Eyre

"Hurt not the earth, neither the sea, nor the trees."
Book of Revelation

"Through a deeper understanding of the relation between earth and cosmos, not only can the soil, plants and animals be healed, but also human life itself."
Stedall

"To look at the world and see it as a unity, to see it whole."
Schumacher

"We need to face up to what we have done. But we also need to remind ourselves of the primal relationship, which contains the possibility of living with trees, and within the whole of nature, lovingly. For if our sense of wonder were once to be awakened, we should no longer be able to act sacrilegiously."
Taplin

"Consider Gaia theory as an alternative to the conventional wisdom that sees the Earth as a dead planet made of inanimate rocks, ocean, and atmosphere, and merely inhabited by life. Consider it as a real [open] system, comprising all of life and all of its environment tightly coupled so as to form a self-regulating entity."
James Lovelock

Bill, Devall comments on and contrasts the dominant Western and now global culture, and that of the Deep Ecology discourse:

Western Culture	Deep Ecology
Dominance over nature	Harmony with nature
Natural environment as a resource for humans	All nature has intrinsic worth and equality
Material / economic growth for growing human population	Elegantly simple material needs (material goals serving the larger goal of self-realisation)
Belief in ample resource reserves	Earth "supplies" limited
High technological progress and solutions	Appropriate technology: non-dominating science
Consumerism	Doing with enough / recycling

He further identifies five key elements in the thought and action of the dominant Western culture:

- There are general assumptions about reality, including man's place in nature.

- There are general "rules of the game" for approaching problems which are generally agreed upon.

- Those who subscribe to a given world view share a definition of the assumptions and goals of their society.

- There is a definite, underlying confidence among believers in the worldview that solutions to problems exist within the assumptions of the worldview [a form of certainty which limits the ability to solve problems, see Stedall p.129].

- Practitioners within the worldview present arguments based on the validity of data as rationally explained by experts.

CULTURAL AND PHILOSOPHICAL PERSPECTIVE

"The truth is so often the reverse of what has been told to us by our culture that we cannot turn our heads far enough around to see it."
Edwards

"Most men lead lives of quiet desperation and go to the grave with the song still in them."
Henry Thoreau

"As one passes from a state of slavery to one of active internal freedom, one experiences joy in one's whole being."
Ludwig Wittgenstein

"As man is, so he sees."
Blake

"For most people, whatever their way of life, the beliefs they accept and utilise are held unselfconsciously and are rarely reflected upon. Moreover, when reflection does occur, it tends merely to depict these beliefs as natural representations of 'how things are'. Critical, analytical examination of beliefs, their origins, functions, and claims to validity, is the province of specialised, academic roles in modern societies, and is a phenomenon of little general significance. The 'Western layman' lives in a taken-for-granted world; solid, objective, and intelligible; on the whole he thinks with his beliefs, but not about them."
Barry Barnes

"Theories reflect their historical context and need therefore to be continually re-evaluated."
Brian Goodwin

"The habits of our culture and the dogmas of our education constrain our sight as they have always done."
Einstein

There are several contrasting viewpoints that are likely to be encountered as we engage with SHE which, whilst they can be viewed as opposites, can also be seen on a continuum oscillating between each pole. I have labelled them with titles that describe the scientific and cultural shift associated with the past 100 years or so:

Hard	Soft
Doing	Being
Rationality	Intuition
Reality	Imagination
Minimal Self	Organic Self
Anthropological	Deep Ecological
Indenture	Freedom
Fragmentation	Holism
Mechanistic	Organic
Knowledge	Wisdom
Answers	Questions
Dominance	Harmony
Control	Flowing
Western Culture	Eastern Culture
Absolute Philosophy	Perennial Philosophy
Objective	Subjective
Inert	Living
Materialism	Spiritualism
Unitary	Plural

Feminine rising

There is much evidence (as cited herein and elsewhere: wars, the climate crisis, pollution, inequality, poverty, industrialisation, dominance of predatory corporate capitalism, globalisation etc.) to show that the past three hundred years or so has been dominated by what we call "masculine" (mechanistic, material centric, ego dominant, power dominant/hungry, competitive, deterministic) energy. In order to rebalance we need an equal pull towards feminine (creative, soul-dominant, healing, caring, nurturing, cooperative, harmonious) energy.

For the first five to six weeks, a human embryo contains only x (female) chromosomes, although some prefer to call this stage "gender neutral". Generally, we tend to say we all start out female (feminine energy dominant). Clearly, by the time we are born we are physically either female or male, but we all have masculine or feminine energies within us to varying degrees, and most of us will have experienced each of these at some point. Indeed, according to ancient Hindu philosophy and yogic teachings it is the dance between these energies that sets the world in harmonious motion, and any imbalance causes conflict, upheaval, and disaster, which much of the world is currently facing.

The importance of the feminine, with its capacity for birth, for bringing the light into the world (also see evolutionary beings above p.61), is well represented in a passage from *Dante's Path* by B & R Schaub:

"In Italian *luce* means "light" and, for Dante, *luce* is the symbol of our human capacity for illumination, for illuminating grace for those experiences of higher consciousness through which we come to see more deeply into reality and even to experience its most cohesive, bonding essence, which is love. Mary is the symbol of that vast [unconditional] love.

In Christianity, Mary is, of course, the mother of the son of God. She is a central figure of the Catholic tradition within which Dante was writing, personifying the creative, compassionate force in the universe. Beautiful and quietly powerful depictions of Mary exist in churches around the world, and even Christians who have left the church retain images of her deep in their psyches. As a symbol of mothering, caring, brave, powerful love, she belongs to a worldwide, ancient, and continuous lineage of figures representing the divine feminine. She is honoured in the Quran of Islam as the mother of one of the prophets (Jesus) and is symbolically identical to the Chinese Buddhist figure of Kuan Yin, the female Buddha of compassion, and to Shechinah, the feminine Hebrew noun for the nurturing aspect of God.

It is encouraging to know that this nurturing, creative, compassionate, and inspiring force is so widely recognised. We all must find a way to remember and honour her in our perception of what is real, because, by whatever name we call her, we are sustained by the fact that she is present in us and in the universe. Knowing that her benevolence is available allows us to accept the challenge of confronting our inner [and outer] hells."

The polarities shown below illustrate some of the attributes of each type of masculine and feminine energy, and we should emphasise the continuous nature between the two poles, the need for integration and the relevance and context of individual subject matter as to the degree of pull towards each pole:

The feminine brings light into the world

FEMININE – MASCULINE
ENERGY POLARITY

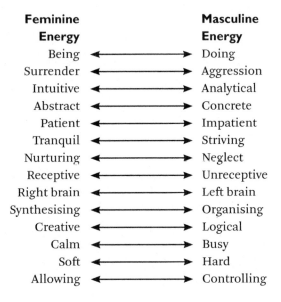

Feminine Energy		Masculine Energy
Being	⟷	Doing
Surrender	⟷	Aggression
Intuitive	⟷	Analytical
Abstract	⟷	Concrete
Patient	⟷	Impatient
Tranquil	⟷	Striving
Nurturing	⟷	Neglect
Receptive	⟷	Unreceptive
Right brain	⟷	Left brain
Synthesising	⟷	Organising
Creative	⟷	Logical
Calm	⟷	Busy
Soft	⟷	Hard
Allowing	⟷	Controlling

The nature of SHE is predominantly associated with feminine energy, and as the challenges of our time have been predominantly caused by masculine energy, the necessary rebalancing energies needed are feminine. It is also important to ensure we don't attribute strength to the masculine or weakness to the feminine. We will need brave males and brave females capable of engaging in each type of energy as and when called for if we are to deliver SHE objectives and return to a harmonious, coherent existence.

The polarities which can be attributed to the pull between masculine and feminine energies, along with their pulls towards other classifications, is provided below:

THE EGO *vs* THE SOUL

Material, superficial. Masculine pull.		Quantum, source. Feminine pull.
Me	*vs*	We
Separation	*vs*	Unity
Blame	*vs*	Understanding
Hostile	*vs*	Friendly
Resentment	*vs*	Forgiveness
Pride	*vs*	Love
Complain	*vs*	Gratefulness
Jealousy	*vs*	Co-happiness
Anger	*vs*	Happiness
Materialism	*vs*	Spiritualism
War	*vs*	Peace
Coldness	*vs*	Sympathy
Past/future-oriented	*vs*	Now oriented
Intolerance	*vs*	Tolerance
Self-importance	*vs*	Togetherness
Egoism	*vs*	Altruism
Self-denial	*vs*	Self-acceptance
Doing	*vs*	Just be

"Be patient toward all that is unsolved in your heart and try to love the questions themselves, like locked rooms and like books that are now written in a very foreign tongue. Do not now seek the answers, which cannot be given you because you would not be able to live them. And the point is, to live everything. Live the questions now. Perhaps you will then gradually, without noticing it, live along some distant day into the answer."
Rilke

ELEMENT FOUR

Now Academy:
helping us to become
what we are meant to be.

To strive, to serve,
to love, to learn.

Seeing the wood
and the trees.
I wonder …

'Theory without practice is empty; practice without theory is blind.''
Immanuel Kant

"You will forget most of what you are forced to memorize in
school. The goal of education, then, is to learn how to think. The
curiosity and enthusiasm of a child is the basic paradigm toward
which all lovers and students of truth must strive. The more
intelligent you are the more intolerable existence becomes."
Gesswein

There will always be more questions than answers, but as I noted on page
4, all the questions are of our own making; it is therefore vital that we consider
them carefully. "Live the questions now" [NOW]. It is vital that we live the
questions in an open, transparent and inquiring manner, not just engage with
them in an academic, theoretical manner. We best learn through experience.

"It takes courage to grow up and become who you really are."
Edward Cummings

"The illiterate of the 21st century will not be those who cannot read
and write, but those who cannot learn, unlearn, and relearn."
Alvin Toffler

Toffler's quotation is critically relevant to our times and all sections of
society including education, business, politics and economics, as we will
increasingly be facing challenges, problems and questions which have never
been previously encountered, especially in respect of technocracy in all its
forms, artificial intelligence, social media, and the climate crisis.

Education, learning, growth and development are all about what we know:
information, knowledge, adopted chosen storyline (social construction). They
are also about our interpretation of the past and present cultural narrative,
and what we don't know: new information, new knowledge, new technologies,
and our ever-emerging new cultural narrative. What we need to develop now is
an advanced cultural narrative, one which is, above all, sustainable, humane,
creative and emergent; learning from the future through better planning and
improved scenario development probably supported by artificial intelligence
and "Intuitive knowledge" (see p.100) so that we can model our ideas, hopes,
values and virtues, thereby hopefully avoiding any existential pitfalls before
we enact them (e.g. those resulting from the industrial and technological
revolutions). Equally, it is about developing our ever-maturing awareness
of our role and impact in evolving our sustainable humanity and making a

valuable contribution to an inclusive liberal and egalitarian society, thereby creating the SHE futures we desire.

The lyrics from "The Waterboys" on p.23 provide a useful introduction and backdrop to the NOW Academy and to the privileged nature of what it truly means to be human: to be in "this special place", our home, planet Earth, to "show our souls", to be who we are meant to be, to "dream", to "play" and "do" here – this is indeed "sacred ground". Don't "bang the drum", don't accept and maintain the status quo like many others do, which can so easily be forgotten as we are indoctrinated into and mesmerised by a socially constructed and increasingly globalised society dominated by a patriarchal, paternalistic ideology, the established socially-constructed human environment, manifested through the legacy of the industrial, technological/information and social-media revolutions. These things, when taken together, can be termed "globalisation", and they threaten all life on Earth – the "sacred ground" – both materially and spiritually.

Choose instead to stand out from the crowd, to think for and be yourself, be who you are meant to be as you seek to contribute to the wellbeing of all – "just to let it come."

Once we overcome the major challenges currently facing us, we can get on with the real work of contributing in a caring, open, humble, creative, liberal, cooperative, "win-win" relationship with all, and with ourselves, in the infinite cosmic unfolding as represented by SHE and enacted through our QED model.

The curiosity and wonder of being human, with our innate awareness, creativity, imagination, and intuition are the source of all that we take to be real; what we call life. These are major themes running through the NOW Academy pedagogy, and they are well represented by the "quantum" metaphor:[38] wholeness, relational, participative, energetic, and creative. Indeed, humans could easily be described as "quantum" beings (relational, observers, participators, and creators) and "quantum" is a useful differentiating label or umbrella under which we will develop, promote and market the NOW Academy offering – QED.

Technological advances have enabled information and knowledge to become freely and readily available. More than half the world's population has access to the Internet. It would therefore be foolish for any educational establishment to continue with an outdated and defunct pedagogy which focuses on regurgitating memorised information and knowledge which is readily available online (through Google and other search engines) and which can only really support and maintain the status quo.

The NOW Academy pedagogy and andragogy applied through our QED model will therefore focus on how to access accumulated information and knowledge, how to expand, critique, build and reframe it, and how to find new sources through developing a creative mindset that utilises imagination, insight, intuition, critical thinking and Action Research (see p.156). From within altruistic mindfulness, the Academy will develop an ever-deepening and emergent understanding of what it means to be human, providing new and deeper insights, but, more importantly, exploring and learning how to utilise them through practice and mastery in order to create and support SHE principles and outcomes and avoid humans becoming purely programmed, manipulated and determined by the output of logical, deterministic algorithms associated with AI[39] and the propaganda from socio-technological and socio-economic landscapes with which we are presented.

In the past twenty years, we have seen the numbers of those attending higher education in the UK doubling. However, on completing their education, many find it difficult to get anything other than low-paid jobs. This leaves them feeling disenfranchised, having been sold the "false" promise of "get a good education and you'll be set for life". The NOW Academy will provide further and higher education for these students, along with a real promise that enable them to put their skills to well-paid use.

A message to all our students and members, of all ages and dispositions:

"Make your lives an incredible journey of infinite potential fuelled by a humane, sustainable and liberal spirit utilising your unique personal gifts, in collaboration with your brothers and sisters, to care for, develop and enhance all our communities, species and our home, planet Earth."

This is worth exploring alongside this question and answer, by all those studying SHE:

SHARED VISION

"What can I do to make my life the greatest use to all life?"
Schmachtenberger

"Make the world work for 100% of humanity, in the shortest possible time, through spontaneous cooperation, without ecological offense or the disadvantage of anyone."
Buckminster Fuller

These quotations well reflect the goal, sentiment and dedication needed for those in the NOW Academy. They lie at the core of our curriculum and are the benchmark for all that we do.

As mentioned earlier, we believe that each person is born into the world for a purpose, bringing unique gifts which unfold over their lifetime. The etymology of the word "education" is the Latin educere, to lead or bring out, to lead or bring out one's unique gifts. The etymology of the word "learning" is from the Gothic, "to find the right track". Thus, bringing and leading our gifts in support of SHE principles and objectives (the right track) resonates with QED ("what was to be shown").

Our students are likely to have been predominantly educated in the historic tradition which Paulo Freire, the Chilean educationalist, refers to as "banking education", in which students are not called upon to know, but to memorise and bank the contents narrated by the teacher, hence making a 'deposit' on which they may "draw" later, to pass exams" (the 19th and 20th Century paradigm). This delivers competence in memory and exam technique, but not competence in dealing with problems, complexity, chaos, relationships, emotional intelligence, wellbeing, or the aesthetic, ethereal, richness (QED) of life as experienced through self-conscious reflection provided in the NOW Academy pedagogy.

Not only will the NOW Academy pedagogy provide such additional competencies through its QED model, but it will also provide a point of reflection from which to compare and contrast the relevance and perspective of two pedagogical schools of thought about education and learning. It will facilitate the bringing out and nurturing of students' unique gifts and contributions.

Whether consciously or unconsciously, we all construct and choose our own unique realities by the way we decide to interpret information, knowledge, our education and experiences, through the relationships we form and maintain and the way we communicate our stories.

Our pedagogical objective is to consolidate an understanding of our current and ever-emerging reality, to critique that understanding, to share it and then to use it as the backdrop before moving forward, through applying SHE principles and the QED model, pedagogy and curriculum, along with NOWs raison d'etre, all of which are founded in the liberal education tradition (global, pluralist, and free), and directed towards a deeper understanding of what it means to be human. This will help us lead the only life we can: our own.

The deeper, richer, and more diverse our exploration through theory, practice and experience – both in terms of understanding our past, our current existence and creating our desired futures (but always from within the ever present now) – the more likely we will be to live wholesome, fulfilled, peaceful and harmonious lives.

Membership of the NOW Academy will reflect a dedication to lifelong learning and continuous personal development by drawing on leading edge thinking in both the sciences and humanities – but, more importantly, through practice and experience. It will provide a clear and accredited (where applicable) differentiation of students' distinctive and emerging gifts, skills, talents, authenticity, professionalism and ecovisionery leadership, embracing both NOW and SHE principles, practices, and objectives.

The following three headings provide useful frameworks for the NOW Academy / SHE content[40] to be taught, understood, challenged, expanded, explored, dialogued, and developed, and to meet the demand of the statement by Kant, above.

ACTION RESEARCH

Explained in A Handbook of Action Research (Reason and Bradbury) as:

"To produce practical knowledge that is useful to people in the everyday conduct of their lives. A wider purpose of action research is to contribute through this practical knowledge to the increased wellbeing – economic, political, psychological, spiritual – of human persons and communities, and to a more equitable and sustainable relationship with the wider ecology of the planet of which we are an intrinsic part. So, action research is about working toward practical outcomes, and also about creating new forms of understanding, since action without reflection and understanding is blind, just as theory without action is meaningless. And more broadly, theories which contribute to human emancipation, to the flourishing of community, which help us reflect on our place within the ecology of the planet and contemplate our spiritual purposes, can lead us to different ways of being together, as well as providing important guidance and inspiration for practice.

The emergent worldview has been described as systemic, holistic, relational, feminine, experiential, but its defining characteristic is that it is participatory: our world does not consist of separate things but of relationships which we co-author. We participate in our world, so that the 'reality' we experience is a co-creation that involves the primal givenness of the cosmos and human feeling and construing."

Such a worldview is very much in keeping with the holistic quantum phenomenon which underlies all, and the postmodern, co-creative perspectives described herein. It allows for multiple perspectives to be developed in participation and harmony with an environment that is as broad as possible, and above all, to understand that it is *our construction* of reality that results, but nonetheless one that we are holding to be real at any given point in time. In essence, Action Research encourages us to constantly inquire into our construction of reality from multiple perspectives through as-broad-as-possible participation, using cycles of action and reflection through experience.

CRITICAL THEORY

"Seeks human emancipation to liberate human beings from the circumstances that enslave them" (Horkheimer 1982, 244). Because such theories aim to explain and transform all the circumstances that enslave human beings, many "critical theories" in the broader sense have been developed. They have emerged in connection with the many social movements that identify varied dimensions of the domination of human beings in modern societies.

In both the broad and the narrow senses, however, a critical theory provides the descriptive and normative bases for social inquiry aimed at decreasing domination and increasing freedom in all their forms." Stanford Encyclopaedia of Philosophy.

In essence, Critical Theory asks us to challenge our taken-for-granted assumptions of how we think, feel, and relate to the world and those around us.

There are similarities to both Action Research and Critical Theory, but the important aspects from my understanding are that they seek to liberate us from the boundaries that we impose or have imposed upon ourselves. They seek an open, transparent, and participative form of inquiry about what is going on, from multiple sources and perspectives. Above all, they contribute to creating a sound foundation for being able to "See the world anew" (Einstein), for encouraging creativity and engaging in an ongoing dialogue – physically, spiritually, epistemologically and ontologically – with all that surrounds us.

DIALOGUE

"Deep conversations with someone who understands you
is everything."
The minds journal.com

Dialogue comes from the Greek (dia-logos) literally "speaking between people". When we have emptied ourselves of all our thoughts, noise and distractions, we listen actively, we clarify, and new understandings emerge. This is Bohm's description of the dialogue process:

"In practical terms, twenty to forty participants sit in a circle for a few hours during regular meetings. This is done with no predefined purpose, no agenda, other than that of inquiring into the movement of thought and exploring the process of "thinking together" collectively. This activity can allow group participants to examine their preconceptions and prejudices, as well as to explore the more general movement of thought. The intention regarding the suggested minimum number of participants was to replicate a social/cultural dynamic (rather than a family dynamic).

Participants in the Bohmian form of dialogue "suspend" their beliefs, opinions, impulses, and judgments while speaking together, in order to see the movement of the group's thought processes and what their effects may be. This kind of dialogue should not be confused with discussion or debate, both of which, says Bohm, suggest working towards a goal or reaching a decision, rather than simply exploring and learning. Meeting without an agenda or fixed objective is done to create a "free space" for something new to happen."

Dialogue, when enacted in a truly open and free-flowing state, allows us to enact our purpose. Dialogue helps us become "Bamboo-like and allows God to flow through us" (Osho, see p.79). We become as one, the same – no boundary, no difference – and once this is realised through embodied empathy, all conflict, derision, questions and differing viewpoints become futile, as there is nothing that separates.

Both dialogue and the description of the creative person mentioned above are well reflected in the following, from Bohm, on dialogue:

"From time to time the tribe gathered in a circle.
They just talked and talked, apparently to no purpose.
They made no decisions.
There was no leader. And everyone could participate.
There may have been wise men or women who were listened to a bit more – the older ones – but everyone could talk.

The meeting went on, until it finally seemed to stop for no apparent reason at all and the group dispersed. Yet after that, everybody seemed to know what to do, because they understood each other so well. Then they could get together in smaller groups and do something or decide things."

The preceding sections will be refined, expanded upon and added to, as part of the design of the curricula to be undertaken within the NOW Academy.

We now turn to perhaps the most important word:

LOVE

"Someday, after mastering the winds, the waves, the tides and gravity, we shall harness for God the energies of love, and then, for a second time in the history of the world, man will have discovered fire."
Pierre Teilhard de Chardin

"When the power of love overcomes the love of power, then we shall know peace."
Jimi Hendrix

Piglet to Winnie the Pooh "Pooh, how do you spell love? Pooh "you don't spell it you feel it."
Alan Milne

Love is no separation. Embracing the subjectivity and sacredness of our existence through the sacrament of love, rather than objectifying and commodifying it out of fear, is an important step towards enlightenment. Love is one of the most subjective of words and is sometimes difficult to describe because it lives in our mental realm, yet we clearly know when it is both present or absent; some speak of it as a third person, an energy or force. I know it is perfect oneness.

We attach such lofty meanings to it: "God is love", Love you forever", "Love conquers all", "Love sets you free". The lyrics from "The power of love" by Frankie Goes to Hollywood elevate it accordingly.

> Love is the light
> Scaring darkness away
> The power of love
> A force from above
> Cleaning my soul
> Love is like an energy
> Rushing in
> Purge the soul
> Make love your goal

along with a few lines from Queen / David Bowie's 'Under Pressure':

Turned away from it all like a blind man
Sat on the fence but it don't work
Keep coming up with love
But it's so slashed and torn
Why can't we give ourselves one more chance
Why can't we give love one more chance
Why can't we give love, give love, give love, give love
'Cause love's such an old-fashioned word
And love dares you to care for
The people on the edge of the night
And love dares you to change our way of
Caring about ourselves.

Shakespeare's Sonnet 116

Let me not to the marriage of true minds
Admit impediments. Love is not love
Which alters when it alteration finds,
Or bends with the remover to remove.
O no! it is an ever-fixed mark
That looks on tempests and is never shaken;
It is the star to every wand'ring bark,
Whose worth's unknown, although his height be taken.

Love's not Time's fool, though rosy lips and cheeks
Within his bending sickle's compass come;
Love alters not with his brief hours and weeks,
But bears it out even to the edge of doom.
If this be error and upon me prov'd,
I never writ, nor no man ever lov'd.

Such lyrics speak for themselves.

Love is power beyond power; it represents the source, our source, the source of everything, perfect oneness. Love is omnipotent, ever present, everywhere and always available to us. However, we can choose to turn towards it, or away from it out of fear of losing our ego, having power over others, self, and greed. It is that which makes us whole: no "he" or "she", "me" or "you", "this" or "that", "in" or "out"... just one, together. We fear we may lose ourselves in love. It is the ego's greatest enemy, and therefore the ego imposes limits and boundaries on love. We try to make it finite (conditional) when in fact it is infinite; in and through love we become who we are meant to be. Love is. God is. God is love, but one can deny such, deny our essential nature and turn away.

Far too often in modern society, love is conditional, finite, seen as a thing or a commodity to be given or withheld, but such conditionality is a contradiction of love – true love can only be unconditional, otherwise it is not love, but something else. The humanist psychologist Carl Rogers offers a useful description when he describes love as "Unconditional positive regard", including genuineness, authenticity, openness, self-disclosure, acceptance, empathy, and approval; unconditional positive regard for everything.

There are many definitions ascribed to love in our modern-day language, but to my mind the three most relevant for NOW come from the ancient traditions in which it could be described as spirit or soul. The first definition comes from the Greek agape, or selfless love.

This was a love that you extended to all people, whether family members or distant strangers. C.S. Lewis referred to it as "Gift love", the highest form of Christian love. But it also appears in other religious traditions, such as the idea of mettā or "universal loving kindness" in Theravāda Buddhism, and in the Islamic Hadith:

"By Him in whose hand my soul is, you will not enter paradise unless you believe, and you will not believe unless you love each other... spread the greetings of peace among you."

Secondly, also from the Greek, Philia concerned the deep comradely friendship that developed between brothers in arms who had fought side by side on the battlefield. It was about showing loyalty to your friends, sacrificing for them, as well as sharing your emotions with them. Thirdly, from the Latin, there is the action of breathing, state of breath, being breathed. Interestingly, the word 'spirit' comes from the Latin 'spiritus' and ultimately from the Old Testament word for spirit, "ruah" both meaning breath. Perhaps it is a gift from God, breath; that which we cannot do without, love; that which we cannot do without, without causing pain.

Everything comes down to the desire of being happy, joyful, content, or at peace (we can use these interchangeably here) and this can only be achieved through love. Happiness is not some transient thing, as we mainly experience in Western culture, associated with material things, but as God, ultimate, infinite, or Spirit (perfect oneness). Whatever the label, it is the peace of being one. In order to find this "happiness", we don't have to do much: we have to engage with love and accept ourselves as we are and who we are able to become. We can choose love.

Love, then, is the central tenet for our SHE/PV programmes, as they direct their attention to the total wellbeing of all. This is encapsulated in the sentiment of something a friend recently said to me: "I want to empower you to make your dreams come true". How awesome would it be if we all embraced such a sentiment to each other; this will certainly be the message we intend to spread throughout the NOW family.

The work to be undertaken by the NOW family from within the NOW Academy is both complex and emergent, but not to be avoided if we are to progress towards enlightenment. It is about everything; we have to consider everything (holism) all of the time to avoid catastrophic unintended consequences such as those that are now being experienced socially, economically and ecologically, and which are very likely to get much worse if we don't. Our ability to model and scenario-plan the complex and emergent forces that are associated with our current challenges and which help us feel our way in to the future, avoiding many potential unintended consequences, will be greatly enhanced through continuing technological and social media development (along with artificial intelligence), rather than just treating the technology as a media plaything to persuade the masses to consume more.

There is both a simplicity and enormity about what we mean by SHE/PV and what we are trying to achieve in the NOW Family because it represents our essential nature   and because we have removed ourselves so far from it, in some sense we need to remember what it means to be human and to paradoxically remember our destiny.

So, the challenge for us is to find our way back home, to our essential nature, to help those lost to it, and to ensure those coming into the world understand and thrive on it. Amoda Maa Jeevan talks about "coming home [to source], awakening [enlightenment] as the beginning not the end, it is the beginning of authentic living:

Living as openness, living as love, living as truth, living as wholeness, when all the illusions, notions of the self and the ego fall away all that remains is love. Not a love that has to do with anything or anyone else, it is a love that recognises love as the inherent nature of everything, everything, both the dark and the light, both the suffering and the bliss, both the mundane and the transcendent. The nature of love is openness, no longer a divide or boundary between you and the totality of life... if there is no separation.

No separation is not about feeling this kind of oneness where we are all connected, it has nothing to do with being connected or disconnected, the whole concept of connectedness just dissolves, and you can only be connected or disconnected if there is still an inner division. Not connected but intimate, life is [truly] experienced in its intimacy; no separation, true coming homeness. You are inseparable from love."

Reflecting on the forgoing, I'm drawn to thinking that much of the content is about how we choose to see ourselves, each other and the world that surrounds us and sustains us. I would like to leave the final words to The Waterboys

I'm gonna look twice at you
Until I see the Christ in you,
When I'm looking through
the eyes of love.

THE WATERBOYS

With love.

Thank you.

Epilogue

Earlier I raised the question "what does it mean to be human".[41] This is a very complex question, but one not to be avoided, either personally and collectively, if we are to survive as a species and as a diverse, stunningly beautiful planet.

We are born of the universe (perfect oneness) as conscious beings to wonder, experience and contribute to the beauty of it all. Currently, we believe, we are likely to be the most intelligent life force in the known universe, and with this comes great responsibility. To use such a position to do harm, control or destroy life in order to achieve our own ends, rather than contribute to its flourishing, has to be insane.

We cannot therefore continue to exploit our home, planet Earth, or that is the end of our story.

From a dualistic perspective, one which I consider to be a wrong turn taken by humankind, we have created two worlds: a human world that is socially constructed, which we can take as either true and real or false and unreal, or anywhere in between. Such a world is heavily influenced by a plethora of government, corporate and social-media propaganda seeking to influence, control, blur and manipulate, and through which it is possible to claim plausible deniability and to rewrite history. And the non-human world, which by definition is everything else. These two worlds are clearly one, and the classifications and separation, into two worlds, into parts, are constructs and perceptions of human minds as they seek their selfish, egotistical ends.

The separation, classification, labelling, deconstruction and resulting simulations and adaptations drawn from our dualistic perceptions and paradigms have resulted in materialism, greed, hedonism, modernity and globalisation, which in turn have produced vast environmental degradation, species extinction, global warming and existential threat for all humankind and our home, planet Earth. However, such circumstances, along with the emergence of quantum phenomena have, to some extent, enabled us to reach a point where we can now recognise the folly of dualism (e.g., the atomic bomb, and global warming to name but two) and allow for a moving-forward in a holistic, caring, and philanthropic manner. Another quote from Bohm illuminates:

"For fragmentation is now very widespread, not only throughout society, but also in each individual; and this is leading to a kind of general confusion of the mind, which creates an endless series of problems and interferes with our clarity of perception so seriously as to prevent us from being able to solve most of them."

Everything is made up from atoms, and – fundamentally – atoms are made up of vibrating energy. In this sense, we and everything around us is related, are remarkably similar, and probably the same at the most fundamental level.

Whether materially, scientifically, socially, or spiritually, we have no way of knowing if what we are taking for granted is anywhere near the truth, unless we continuously, openly and critically appraise and share our awareness's and experiences and find resonance within perfect oneness. Science is a process of investigation and experiment formulated and refined over the past five hundred years or so, and it is what we have convinced ourselves is the most important process we have to understand, but this is not necessarily so. Science believes that because our current theories and experiments seem to work for our current time, current circumstances and chosen perceptions or paradigms, it assumes that these laws were the same billions of years ago and extrapolates them backwards and forwards to create our current picture.

Yet we have no way of ever knowing if this is correct. Indeed, cutting-edge science is challenging this, and totally different laws may have operated billions of years ago. The same goes for social and spiritual laws, and as we continue to learn and evolve, they may well be totally different in the future. "All that can ever really be said is this is how it appears to one at this point in time, but one has no way of truly knowing that in the next second, minute, hour, week, month, year.... that some new information will not be found and everything you previously had thought changes."[42]

Our best barometer is our intuitional holy soul as it draws on the whole panoply of information, awareness, senses, experiences, conscious, sub-conscious and unconscious thoughts, feelings, knowledge and emotions, and draws them into one, second by second, its nature emergent, quantum and holistic.

I am greatly informed, influenced and grateful for all the remarkable insightful quotations included herein, the following being most pertinent at this point: T. Berry, M. Rukeyser, D. Bohm, W. Gitt, E. Tolle, W. Christie, A. Wallace, along with:

"Reality is an adaptive set of perceptions. Perceptions that are there to guide adaptive behaviour they are not there to show you the truth. The perceptions are real as perceptions, we are having our perceptions, but we have assumed there is a pretty tight relationship between our perceptions and reality. Our perceptions are there to hide the truth because the truth [ultimate underlying reality] is too complicated, so we abstract in order to adapt.

You don't see reality you see a user interface. Life is an interface it's just a headset [Artificial Intelligence metaphor] and we construct interfaces [theories etc]. We need to see through these interfaces "as we are lost in the game". Physicists are now saying spacetime is doomed spacetime cannot be fundamental [and spacetime is a taken for granted assumption on which much historical mainstream science was based]" *Hoffman.*

"Who will provide the grand design, what is yours and what is mine. There are no more new frontiers we have got to make it here. We satisfy our endless needs and justify our bloody deeds, in the name of destiny and in the name of God." (The Last Resort, Eagles).

Looking back, how did I get here? How do I know what I know and believe what I believe? Primarily through my awareness, experience, intuition, and choices delivered through my senses and emotions, from within an extremely complex, adaptive, and emergent process of being perpetually in formation (information) flowing. I acknowledge that the resulting, ever-emerging, interpretation, construction, and perception is what I choose to maintain, as what I determine as me, as reality in the ever-emerging and evolving stories (including actions) I tell myself and others. It is vital to the wellbeing of our species and others to ensure that such representations, narratives and actions are authentic and true in order to avoid misrepresenting our role in the great unfolding of the cosmos.

This I know:

"Absolute Power Corrupts Absolutely: Having power corrupts a man, or lessens his morality, and the more power a man has, the more corrupted he will become. This idiom means that those in power often do not have the people's best interests in mind. They are primarily focused on their own benefits, and they may abuse their position of power to help themselves. If you follow the thread that absolute power corrupts absolutely, you can believe that monarchs – those with the most authority – have the most dubious morals. Kinder souls would be found among poorer, less influential people. Naturally, this is not always the case, as there are many examples of kind and good leaders. Of those who are corrupted, it is hard to distinguish whether the power corrupted the man or the men who were drawn to power were already corrupted."[43]

Human reality is a personal experience in awareness determined from a

The act of observation is an act of creation.

HOFFMAN

construction that I make through interpreting my sense perception. As such it is unique to me and not proof of an objective external materially existing reality that remains when I or another human being is not looking. It is a uniquely human experience. Clearly the way we construct and interpret are key to our experience.

Humankind is the intrinsic, elementary (not decomposable), poetic harmony of pure oneness (non-duality). We are the universe evolving and emerging into ever deeper awareness, engaged in a quest to know and experience what we truly are, perfect oneness, no "Me", "You" or "I"; one cosmic soul, one cosmic mind. Only in fragmented minds, fragmented thought and imagination does separation exist; but separation is an illusion, a wrong turn taken by humanity into a cul-de-sac that has imagined a bounded existence of separate, often competing objects, from which all suffering and problems emanate. There is only one problem: that of separation, and the solution is to heal, to make whole.

Deep in our hearts, we know we are one; and in harming, judging, or exploiting others or our home, planet Earth, we are doing so to ourselves. We are abusing ourselves.

We are not taking our existential problems anywhere near seriously enough. Our primary motive must be to greatly limit consumption and hedonic pleasure along with the ownership of assets to a level that is within the earth's ability to thrive, and with the monetary resources saved to provide better for those who are within the lower quartile of income.

On page two, I quoted a passage from Eliot's 'Four Quartets', and as I end, it feels as if I should elaborate:

"Not known because not looked for"

As we have predominantly focused on the ego in an objective, separate, fragmented, modernist scientific paradigm for the past five hundred years or so, and convinced ourselves that we have so much knowledge, we have not looked for the real known.

"But heard, half heard between two waves of the sea..."

This real known – the Truth – is implicit in everything, and we would be able to hear, see and sense it if we gave up our quest for separate knowledge and self-aggrandisement.

"Quick now, here now always..."

There is an urgency for the known – the Truth – to manifest, and this is always the time and place. It always has been and always will be.

"A condition of complete simplicity"

It is so obvious, but we are choosing to overcomplicate and look the other way out of fear and separation, just like the shadows in Plato's allegory of the cave.

"Costing not less than everything"

If we are to truly remember our destiny (perfect oneness), we are going to have to give up all our egotistical illusions of separateness, materialism, predatory competition/capitalism, and greed.

A passage from Elliot's "Choruses from the Rock" illuminates further (see p.111.): "where is the life we have lost in living"?

Too caught up in the process of self-aggrandisement from the allure of a globalised culture fixated on hedonism, greed and consumption, many fail to realise their authentic being is lost in a pathogenic illusion full of false promise.

Imagine if we could condense some or indeed all of the wisdom of some of the great thinkers, poets and musicians of the world into a succinct few paragraphs to guide us into a better now. I've chosen a selection of the quotes and lyrics from some of these herein and expressed them in a few paragraphs below: the italics being my punctuation to help them cohere.

They include: Phil Collins, Jeff Lieberman, REM, Procol Harem, Peter Antony, Edward Bernays, Barry Barnes, Albert Einstein, T.S. Elliott, David Bowie and Queen, David Whyte, St Augustine, Alisa Ramirez, Eckhart Tolle, John Archibald Wheeler, Reason and Bradbury, Max Planck, Jonathan Stedall, Fritjof Capra, Andrew Powell, Pat Thomson, Dermot O'Murchu, Leonardo DaVinci, Jim Al-Khalili, John Barrow and Frank Tipler, James Jeans, Andre Linder, Walter Christie, Nikola Tesla, Kim Taplin and Ron Eyre. So here it is:

"I've been waiting for this moment (*NOW*) for all my life.

I am moving at the speed of light, and I am the age of the universe *but now* see the world is collapsing around our ears *and we are oblivious to its tears, and* although my eyes were open, they might just as well've been closed, it is as if *we* are lost in a fog, as if mesmerised by the allure of the promises *we* have been made *or made to ourselves*.

In almost every act of our daily lives we are dominated by the relatively small number of persons that understand the mental processes of the masses; it is they that pull the wires which control the public mind. The 'Western layman' lives in a taken-for-granted world: solid, objective, and intelligible. On the whole, he thinks with his beliefs, but not about them. The habits of our culture and the dogmas of our education constrain our sight as they have always done. The prevailing economic doctrine (consumerism and globalisation) is pronounced in violent terms: a lie wholly and to the very root. The so-called science of economics is the most cretinous, speechless, paralysing plague.

Where is the life we have lost in living? Where is the wisdom we have lost in knowledge? Where is the knowledge we have lost in information? *We have* turned away from it all like a blind man, sat on the fence but it don't work; deep down we all know it's not alright, the ice is melting.

You must learn one thing; the world was made to be free in, *to become who you are meant to be*. Our whole business in this life is to restore to health, the eye of the heart, to live for someone else, to strive for greatness yet give up everything in an instant for that person. You disappear and then creativity *is*. It's not the physical form we love, but what inhabits the physical form, which is the essence.

The vital act is the act of participation; we participate in our world, so the 'reality' we experience is a co-creation. The mind is the matrix of all; body, soul, spirit and matter they are as inseparable as matter and energy there is only one reality: a complex web of relationships between the various parts of a unified whole.

We are not part of the universe; we are the universe. Everything is process all the way 'down' and all the way 'up', and processes are irreducibly relational. Something much deeper is resurfacing in the emerging consciousness of our time; namely, we are our relationships. We must realise that everything connects to everything else. The atoms that make up my body are identical to the atoms in the rocks and the trees, the air – even the stars – and yet they come together to create a conscious being who can ask the question "what is an atom?" There exists one possible universe designed with the goal of generating and sustaining observers, and the universe thus begins to look more like a giant thought rather than a giant machine. What if our perceptions are as real, or may be, in a certain sense, more real than material objects?

The illusion of separateness we create in order to utter the words "I am" is part of our problem in the modern world. What we now want is closer contact and better understanding between individuals and communities all over the Earth, and the elimination of egoism and pride which is always prone to plunge the world into primeval barbarism and strife.

We need to face up to what we have done. Man was (*is*) to learn from nature (*cosmos*) rather than subdue (*exploit/destroy*) it. Until you're right with the earth nothing can prosper and there's nothing to celebrate. Hurt not the earth, neither the sea, nor the trees.

Knowing and being aware now, we must reverse out of the cul-de-sac recognising ourselves for what we truly are and stop acting sacrilegiously.

Why can't we give ourselves one more chance?

May we all wake up!"

"I shall pass this way but once;
any good that I can do or any
kindness I can show to any
human being [or non-human]; let me do it now.
Let me not defer nor neglect it, for
I shall not pass this way again."
Etienne de Grellet

Be radical, be compassionate, be creative, be giving, be love, be human.

Altogether NOW.

If you would like to know more and engage with NOW, please visit www.nootherway.co.uk.

To be continued.............

NOTES

1 See quote on p.100.
2 Quote from Candles in Babylon, Denise Levertov.
3 See p.145.
4 Jim Al-Khalili extract see p.86.
5 See Hoffman on p.136
6 Heisenberg's Uncertainty Principle states that there is inherent uncertainty in the act of measuring a variable of a particle. Commonly applied to the position and momentum of a particle, the principle states that the more precisely the position is known the more uncertain the momentum is and vice versa.
7 Elif Shafak in an Intelligence[2] video on YouTube 4 August 2019.
8 YouTube video "Warning on China" YouTube 21 August 2019.
9 BBC Pick of the week, 10 January 2021: Colin Murphy, The Late Show on 5 Live.
10 The Guardian, 10 July 2017.
11 Ecovisionary: eco (forging positive, thriving relationships between living things in their environments, home, or society).
12 A mixed economic system is a systemthat combines aspects of both capitalism and socialism.
13 Anthropic Principle states: the universe is in some sense compelled to eventually have consciousness and sapient life emerge within it.
14 See p.32.
15 Forbes.com 25 August 2017.
16 Intelligence[2] on YouTube published on 8 August 2019.
17 Overall processing powers of computers will double every two years.
18 a paradigm of self-indulgence founded upon the notion that we already know best, mechanistic, application of power and control, of cause and effect, prescribed ways of doing, competitive, and separateness.
19 Https://www.usnews.com/news/ Economy/articles/2018-10-17.
20 Https://thehill.com/regulation/ finance 584710-share-of-global-wealth-held-by-Billionaires-climbs-during-pandemic.
21 Https://www.the guardian.com/ environment/2015/jan/15/rate-of-environmental-degradation-puts-life-on-earth-at-risk-say-scientists.
22 Carl Jung, Nietzsche's Zarathustra: notes on the seminar given in 1934-1939. Ed J.L. Jarrett. Princeton University Press, 1988. p.73.
23 See Robert Perry p.125.
24 Also see Hameroff p.133 and Hoffman p.80.
25 The phenomenon in which a wave function dash initially in a superposition of several different possible eigenstates he is to reduce

to a single one of those states after interaction with an observer (a measuring device, or an interaction caused by vibration).

26 Postulated by Hoffman see metaphorabove and p.80 The ego is theicon on the computer screen

27 Extracted and slightly paraphrased from: extracts from everything and nothing: what is nothing? See https://www.dailymotion.com.

28 In physics, action at a distance is the concept that an object can be moved, changed, or otherwise affected without being physically touched buy another object. That is, it is the nonlocal interaction of objects that are separated in space. www.wikipedia.

29 See p.80.

30 As noted in: Justice Mensah & Sandra Ricart Casadevall (reviewing editors) (2019). Sustainable development: meaning, history, principles, pillars, and implications for human action: literature review, cogent social sciences, 5:1, 1653531.

31 An emergent and creative paradigm, relational, participative, holistic, contextual, cooperative.

32 Quantum particles can "know" the states of other quantum particles, even at great distances and correlate their behaviour's with each other instantaneously.

33 Undivided wholeness, everything is in a process of becoming.

34 Explains that a quantum particle does not exist in one state or another, but in all of its possible states at the same time. Observation is needed to collapse the wave function and see the reality office state.

35 Dropping out of a quantum superposition for a moment to use energy to push something around in a classical way.

36 Marks the place where quantum gravity replaces Einstein's relativity.

37 The view all theory that the self is all that can be known to exist.

38 See p.71.

39 Also see The Social Dilemma film on Netflix mentioned earlier.

40 See p.106.

41 See p.65.

42 See p.20.

43 Writing explained.org.

BIBLIOGRAPHY
AND INDEX

A Course in Miracles (Lesson 196), Foundation for Inner Peace, Viking 1975. ISBN 0-670-86975-9. p.119.

A Course in Miracles, Foundation for Inner Peace, Viking 1975. ISBN 0-670 86975 9. p.125.

Al-Khalili, J. See note 27. p.86.

Al-Khalili, J. Atom: The illusion of reality. https://www.youtube.com/watch?v=KFS40iVDeBI. p.132.

Anthony, P. John Ruskin's Labour: A study of Ruskin's social theory, Cambridge University Press 1983. ISBN 978-0-521-08926-5. p.125.

Anthony, P. John Ruskin's Labour: A study of Ruskin's social theory, Cambridge University Press 1983. ISBN 978-0-521-08926-5. p.125.

Attenborough, D, Sir. Speaking at the Royal Geographical Society 15th October 2013. p.49.

Attenborough, D. Sir. https://www.netflix.com/gb/title/80216393. p.140.

Aurobindo, S. As cited in: Where on Earth is Heaven, Jonathan Stedall, Hawthorn Press 2009 p.17. ISBN 978-1-903548-90-7. p.77.

Bannon, S. Warning on China, YouTube 21st August 2019. p.32.

Barnes, B. Scientific Knowledge and Sociological Theory, Routledge & Kegan Paul 1974. ISNB 0-7100-7962-1. p.143.

BBC pick of the week 10 Jan 2021: Colin Murphy, The Late Show on 5 Live. p.32

Behling, D. Professor. As reported in: On Studying the Humanities: what does it mean to be human, The Huffington Post 6thMay 2012. p.119.

Bergson, H. As cited in: Where on Earth is Heaven, Jonathan Stedall, Hawthorn Press 2009 p.18. ISBN 978-1-903548-90-7. p.90.

Bernays, E. Propaganda. 1928. 2004 edition ISBN 9780970312594. p28.p.50.

Berry, T. The Dream of the Earth, Thomas Berry, Sierra Club Books 1990 ISBN0-87156-622-2. p.9.

Berry, T. The Dream of the Earth. Sierra club books 1990. ISBN 0-87156-622-2. p.31.

Berry, T. The Dream of the Earth, Thomas Berry, Sierra Club Books 1990 ISBN0-87156-622-2. p.36.

Berry, T. The Dream of the Earth, Thomas Berry, Sierra Club Books 1990 ISBN0-87156-622-2. p.127.

Black Elk. https://en.wikipedia.org/wiki/Black_Elk p.106.

Blake, W. https://en.wikipedia.org/wiki/The_Doors_of_Perception. p.83.

Blake, W. p.143.

Bohm, D. Thought as a system. Routledge 1992. ISBN 0-415-11030-0. p.20.

Bohm, D. Wholeness and Implicate Order, Routledge 1998. ISBN 0-415-11966-9. p.79.

Bohm, D. Infinite Potential: The life and times of Bohm, D. Peat, Helix Books 1997. ISBN 0-201-32820-8. p.85.

Bohm, D. Thought as a system, Bohm, Routledge 1994. ISBN 978-0-415110-30-3. p.97/98.

Bohm, D. Thought as a system. Routledge 1992 p Forward x. ISBN 0-415-11030-0. p.124.

Bohm, D. Wholeness and the Implicate Order, Routledge 1980. ISBN 0-415-11966-9. p.137.

Bohm, D. http://www.insightexpedition.com/bohmian_dialogue.html. p.158.

Bohm, D. As cited in: Honoured Feathers of Wisdom, Boggs, R Ph.D. iUniverse Inc 2003. ISBN 0-595-66104-1. p.158.

Bohm, D. Wholeness and Implicate Order, Routledge 1998. ISBN 0-415-11966-9. p.165.

Bohme, J. p.137.

Book of Revelation. p.141.

Buddha. Source: The Dhammapada, translated by Juan Mascaro, Penguin Classics 2015. ISBN 978-0141398817. p.8.

Burke, E. In a letter addressed to Thomas Mercer: Thoughts on the Cause of the Present Discontents (1770). p.64.

Capra, F. The Web of Life, Flamingo 1997. ISBN 0-00-654751-6. p.136.

Carney, M. BBC Radio 4 Today programme 30 December 2019. p.12.

Carville, J. https://en.wikipedia.org/wiki/It%27s_the_economy,_stupid p.109.

Chatelet, E. https://en.wikipedia.org/wiki/%C3%89milie_du_Ch%C3%A2telet. p.86.

Chew, G. As cited in: Where on Earth is Heaven, Jonathan Stedall, Hawthorn Press 2009 p.305. ISBN 978-1-903548-90-7. p.80.

Chopra, D. YouTube video: What did George Harrison know https://www.youtube.com/watch?v=SF4OxulBDuk p.81.

Christian Bible, Corinthians 13:12. p.63.

Christie, W. As cited in: Nature-guided Therapies, Brief Integrated Strategies for Health and Wellbeing. p.120.

Clark, L. As cited in: Where on Earth is Heaven, Jonathan Stedall, Hawthorn Press 2009 ISBN 978-1-903548-90-7. p.27.

Credit Suisse global wealth report 2019. p.10.

Cummings, E. p.152.

Dante. The Divine Comedy. P16.

DaVinci, L. p.139.

Devall, B. Deep Ecology: living as if the natural world matters, Devall, Sessions, Gibbs Smith 1984. ISBN 0-87905-247-3. p.142.

Durning, A. How Much is Enough? The Consumer Society and the Future of the Earth, W.W. Norton Company 1992. ISBN 978-0-393308-91-4. p.122.

Eagles. The Last Resort (Henley, Frey). Hotel California Album 1976. p.166.

Edwards, D. Free to be human, Green Books 1995. ISBN 1-870098-88-9. p.55.

Edwards, D. Free to be human, Green Books 1995. ISBN 1-870098-88-9. p.143.

Einstein, A. https://archive.nytimes.com/www.nytimes.com/books/99/05/16/specials/einstein-ideas.html. p.95.

Einstein, A. p.143.

Einstein, A. p.157.

Eliot, T.S. Four Quartets, p.222,3, Collected Poems 1909-1962. ISBN 0-571054-83. p.1.

Eliot, TS. Choruses from 'The Rock' 1 p.161, Collected Poems 1909-1962. ISBN 0-571054-83. p.111.

Exodus 3:14. p.29.

Eyre, R. As cited in: Where on Earth is Heaven, Jonathan Stedall, Hawthorn Press 2009 p.281. ISBN 978-1-903548-90-7. p.141.

Eysteinsson, T. www.humansandnature.org/what-does-it-mean-to-be-human. p.72.

Fox, W. Towards a transpersonal ecology: developing new foundations for environmentalism, Shambhala. ISBN 0-7914-2775-7. p.50.

Frankie Goes to Hollywood. © Perfect Songs Ltd., Gaucho Music Publ. Corp., Perfect Songs Ltd. https://www.youtube.com/watch?v=NyoTvgPnorU. p.159.

Freire, P. http://puente2014.pbworks.com/w/file/fetch/87465079/freire_banking_concept.pdf. p.155.

Freud, S. As cited in: Indifferent Boundaries: Spatial Concepts of Human Subjectivity, Kirby, K. The Guilford Press1996. ISBN 0-89862-572-6. p.121.

Friedman, T. YouTube Intelligence2 video 8th August 2019. p.52.

Fuller, B. As cited in: End of Ignorance: The Strategic Emergence of New Virtual School, Charles B. Winborne, iUniverse Inc 2003. ISBN 0-595-27743-8. p.154.

Gandhi. p.49.

Genis, M. https://www.latest.facebook.com/CanadianPaganSpiritualists/posts/2690607087644481. p129.

Gerber, J. As cited in: Where on Earth is Heaven, Jonathan Stedall, Hawthorn Press 2009 p.18. ISBN 978-1-903548-90-7. p.90.

Gesswein, A. Ethics: maxims and reflections. ISBN-13: 978-0692812679. p.36.

Gesswein, A. Ethics: maxims and reflections. ISBN-13: 978-0692812679. p.124.

Gesswein, A. Ethics: maxims and reflections. ISBN-13: 978-0692812679. p.152.

Gesswein, A. Ethics: maxims and reflections. ISBN-13: 978-0692812679. p.141.

Gitt, W. In the Beginning Was Information, Master Books 2006. ISBN 0890514615. p.93.

Gliser, M. https://www.npr.org/sections/13.7/2011/01/19/133037010/searching-for-the-essence-of-physical-reality p.136.

Goethe, J. p.14.

Goethe, J. p.86.

Goethe, J. p.106.

Goethe, J. p.137.

Goodwin, B. As cited in: Where on Earth is Heaven, Jonathan Stedall, Hawthorn Press 2009 p.413. ISBN 978-1-903548-90-7. p.143.

Green, J. As cited in: a series broadcast on BBC iPlayer: Looking for Alaska. p.92.

Greenpeace USA. https://greenpeaceusa.tumblr.com/post/93508666790/the-earth-is-46-billion-years-old-scaling-to-46. p.9.

Grellet, S. https://www.passiton.com. P171.

Griffiths, B. Lord. Extract from The Times newspaper 13th July 2009. p.59.

Gurria, A. OECD Secretary General, 21 May 2015. p.10.

Guterres, A. UN Secretary General. 18 July 2020. p..10

Hameroff, S. Quantum Consciousness, Quantum mind Part 1-2. https://www.youtube.com/watch?v=OEpUIcOodnM&t=386s https://www.youtube.com/watch?v=6kQYPSD6t6c&t=154s p.133

Harding, S. www.humansandnature.org/what-does-it-mean-to-be-human. P.70.

Heisenberg, W. https://en.wikipedia.org/wiki/Uncertainty_principle. p.79.

Hendrix, J. https://en.wikiquote.org/wiki/Sri_Chinmoy. p.159.

Heraclitus. p.86.

Hesse, H. Steppenwolf, translated by Thomas Wayne, Algora Publishing 2010. ISBN 978-0-87586-783-0. p.128.

Hillman, J. The essential James Hillman: A blue fire. Routledge 1990. ISBN 978-0- 415-05303-7. p.18.

Hoffman, D. Reality is Not as it Seems, The New York Academy of Science https://www.youtube.com/watch?v=3MvGGjcTEpQ&t=1659s p.130.

Hoffman, D. https://en.wikipedia.org/wiki/Dold Hoffman Conscious Realism. p.136.

Hoffman, D. Humans ar detached from reality, Donald Hoffman and Lex Fridman https://www.youtube.com/watch?v=nM_FOUCpJ3I&t=791s. p.166.

Hughes, B. The Hemlock Cup: Socrates, Athens and the Search for the Good Life. Vintage Books 2011 ISBN 9780224071789. p.15

Hutchins. G. video: www.youtube.com/watch?v=t2mUebq5PXU&feature=youtu.be. p.65.

Indian Journal of Psychiatry, January 2013. p.94.

Islamic Hadith. p.161.

James, W. As cited in: Where on Earth is Heaven, Jonathan Stedall, Hawthorn Press 2009 p.18. ISBN 978-1-903548-90-7. p.90.

Jeevan, A. Deep intimacy with what is. https://www.youtube.com/watch?v=zE2A1KEQ_lo. p.162.

Jung, C. As cited in: Evolutionary Faith: Rediscovering God in Our Great Story, O'Murchu, D, Orbis Books 2002. ISBN 1-57075-451-9. p.61.

Jung, C. https://www.thesap.org.uk/articles-on-jungian-psychology-2/carl-gustav-jung/jungs-model-psyche/. p.68.

Jung, C. As cited in: Environmental Virtue Ethics, Cafaro, P and Sandler, R, Rowan, and Littlefield Publishers 2005 p.66. ISBN-13 978-0742533899. p.73.

Jung, C. As cited in: Exploring the Collective Unconsciousness in the Age of Digital Media, Stephen,

Brock Shaffer, IGI Global 2016. ISBN 97814666989 18. p.113.

Kant, I. p.152.

Krishnamurti, J. https://jkrishnamurti.org/schools. p.105.

Kubler-Ross. E. https://en.wikipedia.org/wiki/K%C3%BCbler-Ross_model. p.110.

Kumar, S. From a talk given at Lancaster University 1999. p.81.

Lasch, C. The minimal self, W.W. Norton & Co 1984. ISBN 928-0-3932-4836-1. p.50.

Levertov, D. Candles in Babylon, as quoted in: Transforming Terror: Remembering the Soul of the World by. p.19.

Lewis, C. The Four Loves, Harper Collins 1960. ISBN 978-0-00-746122-6. p.161.

Lieberman, J. www.youtube.com/watch?v=No--_R6xThs. p.36.

Lieberman, J. www.youtube.com/watch?v=No--_R6xThs. p.68.

Lissau, R. As cited in: Where on Earth is Heaven, Jonathan Stedall, Hawthorn Press 2009 p.268. ISBN 978-1-903548-90- 7. p.124.

Lovell, B. As cited in: Where on Earth is Heaven, Jonathan Stedall; Hawthorn Press 2009 p253. ISBN 978-1-903548-90-7. p.139.

Lovelock, J. As cited in: Global Intelligence and Human Development: toward an ecology of global learning. p.141.

Mate, G. YouTube: TEDx Rio+20: https://www.youtube.com/watch?v=66cYcSak6nE. p.62.

Mensah, J. & Ricart, S. Casadevall (Reviewing editor) (2019) Sustainable development: Meaning, history, principles, pillars, and implications for human action: Literature review, Cogent Social Sciences, 5:1, 1653531. p.118.

Milne, A. Classic Winne the Pooh. p.159.

Naess, A. As cited in: Uncovering and Discovering the Key to Spiritual Growth: Personal, Peace, Love and the survival of the Planet, Kae, R, Author House 2004. ISBN 1-4184-0673. p.141.

Naisbitt, J. www.youtube.com/watch?v=t2mUebq5PXU&feature=youtu.be. p.65.

NASA global climate changes report. P10.

Native American saying. p.109.

O'Donohue, J. Divine beauty: the invisible embrace. Bantam Press 2003. 0-593046-102. p.22.

O'Donohue, J. https://www.mindfulnessassociation.net/words-of-wonder/for-presence-john-odonohue. p.113.

O'Murchu, D. Rev. Quantum Theology: Spiritual Implications of the New Physics, Crossroad Publishers 2004. ISNN 9780824522636. p.80.

O'Murchu, D. Quantum Theology: Spiritual Implications of the New Physics, Crossroad Publishers 2004. ISNN 9780824522636. p.139.

Oriah Mountain Dreamer. The invitation. http://www.oriahmountaindreamer.com/ index.php. p.40.

Osho. Creativity: Unleashing the Forces Within, St Martin's Griffin 1999 p.146. ISBN 0-312-20519-8. p.79.

Osho. Creativity: Unleashing the Forces Within, St Martin's Griffin 1999 p.146. ISBN 0-312-20519-8. p.96.

Osho. Sex Matters: From Sex to Super-consciousness, St Martin's Griffin 2002 p.22. ISBNo-312-31630-5. p.120.

Ourworlddata.org. p.10.

Parmenides. https://sevencircumstances.com. p.86.

Perry, R. https://circleofa.org/. P.125.

Planck, M. https://en.wikiquote.org/wiki/ p.95.

Powell, A. As cited in: Where on Earth is Heaven, Jonathan Stedall, Hawthorn Press 2009 p.317. ISBN 978-1-903548-90-7. p.137.

Procol Harum. A whiter shade of pale. p.123.

Propaganda of Consumerism. https://www. youtube.com/watch?v=8l5fRI-YnGo. p.51.

Queen / David Bowie. Under Pressure© Sony/ATV Music Https://www.youtube.com/watch?v=NukVyrhQ9cA ublishing LLC, Tintoretto Music . . p.159.

Quran (10:57). p.63.

Ramirez, A. www.humansandnature.org/what-does-it-mean-to-be-human. p.72.

Reason and Bradbury. A Handbook of Action Research, Sage Publications 2001. ISBN 1-4129-2030-2. p.156.

Rilke, M. Selected poems, trans. Robert Bly, Harper, and Row 1981. ISBN 978-1-439-

51010-0. p.17.

Rilke, M. p.149.

Rogers, C. Freiberg, H. Freedom to Learn, Prentice Hall 1994. ISBN 0-02-403121-6. p.104.

Rogers, C. https://en.wikipedia.org/wiki/ Unconditional_positive_regard. P161.

Roszak, T. As cited in: Where on Earth is Heaven, Jonathan Stedall, Hawthorn Press 2009. ISBN 978-1-903548-90-7. p.121.

Rukeyser, M. The speed of darkness. https://en.wikiquote.org/w/ index.php?title=Muriel_ Rukeyser&oldid=2592331. p.30.

Schaub, B&R. Dante's Path: A Practical Approach to Achieving Inner Wisdom, Penguin Group, 2003. ISBN 1-59240-029-9. p.146.

Schmachtenberger, D. Explaining the Facebook Files (Wall Street Journal) www.youtube.com/ watch?v=LmlbhD6LbSA&t=2143s. p.54.

Schmachtenberger, D. YouTube video. P154.

Schopenhauer, A. p.47.

Schumacher, E. Small is Beautiful: A Study of Economics as if People Mattered, Vintage Books 1993 p59. ISBN 9780099225614. p.55.

Schumacher, E. As cited in: Where on Earth is Heaven, Jonathan Stedall, Hawthorn Press 2009 p.281. ISBN 978-1-903548-90-7P71. p.141.

Shafak, E. YouTube video by Intellignce2, 4thAugust 2019. p.32.

Shakespeare, W. P6. The seven ages. Shakespeare, W. Sonnet 116. p.160.

Smolin, L. YouTube video, The RSA: A new theory of time, 24th July 2013. p.68.

Snyder, G. As cited in: The Cultures of the American West, Neil Campbell, Fitzroy Dearborn Publishers 2000. ISBN 1-57958-288-5. p.114.

Socrates. P15.

Socrates p.113.

Spira, R. https://www.inspiringquotes.us/ quotes/Z5NP_jqJxHvuc. p.37.

Spira, R. https://www.youtube.com/ watch?v=wvtsXkNDQv4. p.76.

Spira, R. p.84.

St Francis of Assisi. P.68.

St Augustine. p.70.

Stanford University: http://shc.stanford. edu/what-are-the-humanities. p.119.

Stanford Encyclopaedia. https://stanford. library.sydney.edu.au/archives/fall2008/ entries/critical-theory/ p.157.

Stapp, H. https://en.wikipedia.org/wiki/ Henry_Stapp. p.120.

Stedall, J. Where on Earth is Heaven, Jonathan Stedall, Hawthorn Press 2009. ISBN 978-1-903548-90-7. p.90.

Stedall, J. Where on Earth is Heaven, Jonathan Stedall, Hawthorn Press 2009. ISBN 978-1-903548-90-7. p.101.

Stedall, J. Where on Earth is Heaven, Jonathan Stedall, Hawthorn Press 2009. ISBN 978-1-903548-90-7. p.124.

Stedall, J. Where on Earth is Heaven, Stedall, Hawthorn Press 2009. ISBN 978-1-903548-90-7. p.128.

Stedall, J. Where on Earth is Heaven, Jonathan Stedall, Hawthorn Press 2009. ISBN 978-1-903548-90-7. p.129.

Stedall, J. Where on Earth is Heaven, Jonathan Stedall, Hawthorn Press 2009. ISBN 978-1-903548-90-7. p.129.

Stedall, J. Where on Earth is Heaven, Jonathan Stedall, Hawthorn Press 2009. ISBN 978-1-903548-90-7. p.129.

Stedall, J. Where on Earth is Heaven, Jonathan Stedall; Hawthorn Press 2009 p221 and 122. ISBN 978-1-903548-90-7. p.139.

Stedall, J. Where on Earth is Heaven, Jonathan Stedall; Hawthorn Press 2009 p221 and 122. ISBN 978-1-903548-90-7. p.141.

Steiner, R. As cited in: Where on Earth is Heaven, Jonathan Stedall, Hawthorn Press 2009 p.76. ISBN 978-1-903548-90-7. P.68.

Stout, L. The shareholder value myth: https:// scholarship.law. cornell.edu/cgi/viewcontent. cgi?article=2311&context=facpub. p.58.

String Theory. www.youtube.com/ watch?v=eGxPGgPdTVw. And www. youtube. com/watch?v=yoUcrGncBTo. p.79.

Suzuki, D. The Sacred Balance Rediscovering Our Place in Nature, Greystone Books 1997 p.275. ISBN 978-1-55365-166-6. p.123.

Suzuki, D. The Sacred Balance Rediscovering Our Place in Nature,

Greystone Books 1997 p.287.

ISBN 978-1-55365-166-6. p.124.

Taoist saying. p.129.

Taplin, K. Tongues in trees: studies in literature and ecology, Green Books 1989. ISBN 1-870098-22-6. 100.

Taplin, K. Tongues in trees: studies in literature and ecology, Green Books 1989. ISBN 1-870098-22-6. p.117.

Taplin, K. Tongues in trees: studies in literature and ecology, Green Books 1989. ISBN 1-870098-22-6. p.141.

Teilhard de Chardin, P. As cited in: Prayers to an Evolutionary God, W. Cleary, Sky Paths Publishing 2004. ISBN 1-59473—006-7. p.159.

Tennyson, Alfred Lord. P11.

Theravāda Buddhism. p.161.

Tesla, N. As cited in: The Einstein Illusion, The infirmity of modern physics, Samuel, Luis, Dael, Vision Impact Publishing 2010. ISBN 978-0-9827131-0-7. p.78.

Tesla, N. tps://www.goodreads.com/quotes/308834 p.129.

Thomson, E. Mind in Life – Biology, Phenomenology, and the Sciences of Mind (Cambridge MA: Belknap Press of Harvard University Press, 2007) p137.

Thoreau, H. p.143.

Tocqueville, A. Democracy in America (1865). p.51.

Toffler, A. As cited in: Oxford Essential Quotations (4 ed.), S. Ratcliffe, Oxford University Press 2016. ISBN 9780191826719. p.152.

Tolle, E.What Happens When We Die. www.youtube.com/ watch?v= Vk14R4A_p9w. p.92.

Tolle, E. As cited in; The Real Me, Find and Express Your Authentic Self, Mark Eyre, Business Expert Express 2017. ISBN 978-1-63157-703-1. p.124.

The Minds Journal. https://themindsjournal. com. p.157.

The Social Dilemma. https://www.netflix.com/gb/title/81254224. p.32.

The Waterboys. www.mikescottwaterboys.com/waterboys-lyrics.php. Don't Bang the Drum lyrics © Welk Music Group Ltd., Dizzy Heights Music Publishing, Ltd. p.23.

The Waterboys. The Christ in You. © Pucksongs, Pucksongs - Catalogue

https://www.youtube.com/ watch?v=skgqieCwZRA. p.163.

Twain, M. https://marktwainstudies.com/ p.113.

UN.org. p.44.

USNews.com. https://www.usnews.com/news/economy/articles/2018-10-17/world- bank-half-the-world-lives-on-less-than- 550-a-day. p.55.

Wagoner. D. As cited in: The heart aroused by Whyte, D. Currency Doubleday 1994 p.259. ISBN0-385-42350-0. p.33.

Wagoner, D. As cited in: The heart arouse by Whyte, D. Currency Doubleday 1994 p.259. ISBN0-385-42350-0. p.84.

WSJ.com (Wall Street Journal). 14 September 2021. p.57.

Wallace, A. Video. https://www.youtube.com/ watch?v=pLbSlCoPucw. p.132.

Walsch, N. D. When Everything Changes Change Everything: In a Time of Turmoil Chose a Pathway to Peace, EmNin Books 2009. ISBN 978-1-57174-606-1. p.136.

Watson, G. The Mystery of Physical Life, Lindisfarne Press 1992. ISBN 0-940262-53-3. p.80.

Watson, G. The Mystery of Physical Life, Lindisfarne Press 1992. ISBN 0-940262-53-3. p.139.

Wei Wu Wei. www.goodreads.com/quotes/540671. p.66.

Wheeler, J. https://en.wikipedia.org/wiki/Wheeler%27s_delayed-choice_experiment.p.79.

Wheeler, J. As cited in: In the Spirit of Hegel, Solomon, R, Oxford University Press 1985. ISBN 0-19-503650-6. p.137.

Whyte, D. Sweet Darkness, The House of Belonging, May Rivers Press 1997. ISBN 0-9621524-3-9. p.113.

Williams, W. As cited in: The heart aroused, David Whyte, Currency Doubleday 1994. ISBN0-385-42350-0. p.105.

Winnicott, D. Playing and Reality, Donald Winnicott, Routledge New York 1990. ISBN 0-415-03689-5. p.64.

Wittgenstein, L. P143.

World Economic Forum. Stephane Kasriel: The future or work, gender and education. p.65.

World Commission on Environment and Development, 1987. p.118.

Wwwf.panda.org. p.10.